THE
WISDOM
OF DOING THINGS
WRØNG

Surprising Insights From
An Unusual Approach

RON DONOVAN

The Wisdom of Doing Things Wrong

Pencairn Publishing, Box 1235, Freeland, WA 98249 USA

For information about special discounts available for bulk purchases, sales promotions, fundraising, and educational needs, contact Pencairn Publishing at Pencairn.com.

Visit the author's website at RonDonovan.com

First Edition

ISBN-9780997676303

10   9 8 7 6 5 4 3 2 1

To my wife, Lynne Donnelly

You have been my editor, supporter, critic,
and friend for almost 40 years. Without your advice
and insistence, this book would still be in my head.

Thank you, darling.

Acknowledgements

All my life I have learned from and been amazed by the people I have met. To each of the unnamed people in this book, thank you. If you recognize yourself, I hope you are pleased with the story.

BRIDGET SMITH, you gave valuable time and insight to the design of the book and its cover. You are also my oldest friend on the planet. Thank you, dear.

RUTH MOTT, you took a chance on a guy in a bird costume and started a long friendship. Thank you for your coaching, compassion, and keen writer's eye.

DON ARNOUDSE, you have been a friend and mentor for decades. It was your confidence and ultimatum that got me involved in my consulting and education career. Thank you, Don.

JIM CHAMPY, you are in this book. But you deserve a book of your own for your gentle and powerful approach when assembling and leading a group of diverse thinkers and doers. Jim, you have given me more than I have ever been able to thank you for.

GLENN MANGURIAN, you have been a mentor and an example of how to live a life from the moment I first met you. You have no idea how often I refer to your wisdom, my friend.

BOB DANTOWITZ, you introduced me to some of the magic behind business success. Your playful nature and keen eye for talent taught me a lot about what truly makes an organization work. It has been a joy, Bob.

PETER HOMA, you are an inspiration and a model of how CEOs can and should work. Your combination of humane demands, clear thinking, and unwarranted optimism always got the job done. You have taught me a lot.

CHUCK GIBSON, you have been my friend and teacher for all of my consulting career. I have always stood in awe of your vast knowledge, your enthusiasm, and your ability to lead a case discussion. I appreciate you, Chuck.

SHAE HADDEN, you are my friend and editor and coach. You had an expectation that this book would be finished and now it is. Your editing and writing wisdom helped make it possible. Thank you, Shae.

Contents

Foreword

WORKING WITH YOURSELF (CHAPTERS 1 THROUGH 9)

The world is marvelous and crazy. And our time here is short.

You can either move toward the life you want or away from it. If you want to lead your own life, the life that is uniquely yours to live, you have to start with yourself. The world — and your life — doesn't change until you do. And change starts by looking at what you think and how you look at things.

You can be your own best friend or your own worst enemy.

WORKING WITH OTHERS (CHAPTERS 10 THROUGH 21)

No matter how good you are, you're going to need the help of others to accomplish your goals. How you think, talk, and act influence how others act toward you and whether they are willing to help.

Other people are just like us in that they have moments when they are kind, brilliant, and generous. And they, like us, can be angry, short-sighted, and lazy.

We can't make anyone change. But we can make small changes in how we act toward others. That, alone, can change the world.

▶

WORKING WITH ORGANIZATIONS (CHAPTERS 22 THROUGH 43)

The larger the organization, the more we tend to moan about how difficult it is to change and how we would be better off on our own. There are some organizations that will never change, but you won't know for sure until you try.

Whenever I despair about the possibility of improvement, I think about cigarettes. When I was young, it was clear the tobacco companies controlled the message and the Congress. People could, and did, smoke anywhere. And then things changed.

Not overnight, but slowly and inevitably.

We start small and change big.

CHAPTER 1

There is Wisdom in Doing Things Wrong

We have big changes to make. But although big change is almost impossible, effective change is not. Effective change is a lot of little change happening so quickly it looks like big change. And this we know how to do.

It starts at a personal level. We see a problem and, at the same time, we see a solution. We know we could lead this change, but too often we don't. Too often we remain silent. The reason it doesn't happen for most of us is that very small change can feel wrong. Just try to brush your teeth or write your name with your other hand. Unless you have some compelling reason, like a broken wrist, you'll quickly go back to what you've always done. We can't keep doing what we've always done anymore.

History has proven, even in the face of existential threats, humanity prefers familiarity to change. We cling and return to comfortable ways of doing and thinking even when those ways are a threat. According to a recent Gallup poll, 70% of people are not engaged with their work. Of that number, 20% are actively disengaged. That's not healthy for the workers or the companies.

Outside of work, more and more people are lonely, depressed, and isolated. That's not healthy at all.

The only way we can push through the unworkable habits of our past toward a thriving future is by doing new and uncomfortable things. There is wisdom in doing things in a way that feels wrong. And it is the responsibility of each of us to start. We don't need to wait until we are in positions of power or until we have enough money to buy a solution. We need to start right now wherever we are.

Once it was enough for a few leaders to stand in the river and attempt to change its course. Some of those leaders would be listened to and most would be destroyed by the current of majority opinion.

We now need many more leaders. Our challenges demand many more women and men who have the courage to go against a flow they know doesn't work. We need them to stand together and divert the river to a channel that honors our humanity and our planet. We need to move toward a way of living and working that honors the components of life that we might consider on our deathbeds. We need to preserve our home planet so our great-grandchildren can bask in its beauty and its ability to sustain and delight us.

This kind of change starts with each of us. To change the world, our organization, or our family, we must first change ourselves. We, in our hearts, have to be comfortable knowing that our discomfort with being in the wrong is worth it for creating the life we want to live in the society we want to live in.

You can start by just changing one small habit that bothers only you. I recommend a one-degree change. You don't need to change the entire habit, just change one degree. Perhaps you procrastinate, for example. There may be 10 activities your procrastination affects. Just change one of them for 30 days. If you procrastinate on doing required reading, preparing strategies, meeting with people you don't want to meet with, and doing the dishes, just do the dishes without procrastinating for 30 days. See how it makes you feel.

If you feel good about it, select the next thing you procrastinate on and do both the dishes and that thing for another 30 days. With this approach, in six months you will have changed six habits in a major way.

This model works for any big change. Pick a small piece of a big problem and work on it. Then, even if you haven't completely finished, add another small piece. A lot of people doing this delivers huge results.

Many organizations don't start down the path of real change because they are afraid of getting it wrong. They are afraid of looking silly, of wasting money, of using up the goodwill of the people who have to implement the change. We know how to avoid these problems. All we have to do is focus the change to benefit the employees' ability to do the job they want to do. We give them the tools, they make the changes. The changes are based on a safe approach, quick benefits, and a control and authority that employees seldom get. Once they have started improving their own lives — and the lives of the people around them — they will not stop. And the people around them, their colleagues, will see the benefit and demand that they be allowed to improve their own situation.

We need to be aware of the limiting power of a few myths about change.

MYTH NUMBER ONE: SOMEBODY KNOWS WHAT TO DO

There is a feeling in organizations that somebody knows the right thing to do to fix this mess. But in fact nobody knows what to do. It's too complex, it's too scary to even try some of the ideas. If we work together, it is possible to figure out.

MYTH NUMBER TWO: PEOPLE DON'T LIKE CHANGE

People love change. If they didn't, there would be no travel industry, no fashion industry, no interior paint industry. People wouldn't change cities, jobs, or partners. We love change. But it has to be change we understand and agree with. We must also have a hand in creating the change and controlling it.

MYTH NUMBER THREE: WHATEVER IS GOOD FOR THE COMPANY IS GOOD FOR THE PEOPLE

This may be true for some places, but what is more true is that what is good for the people is good for the company. Which one of these offers is most likely to be accepted by an employee? "We have found a new way to make you more efficient to save time and money for the organization" or "Would you like to learn some simple, flexible tools that would make your job easier and lower your level of exhaustion, frustration, and despair?"

We know how to do this. It's simple enough that you do not need consultants, you do not need to send people away for education, you do not need to spend a lot of money or time before you start saving a lot of money and time. All you have to do is begin where you are.

The following are ideas I want to share with you with the hope you'll see some of your own issues and decisions in a different light. Some are emotional and some are prescriptive. I hope you find all of them useful.

CHAPTER 2

What If Tomorrow Isn't Another Day?

We wonder sometimes if we're enough. Why should we be the ones to take a risk, to lead a team, to challenge convention? What do you intend to leave behind? If you want to leave something useful, start today. There is no guarantee of tomorrow. People who lead change live like there's no tomorrow.

When I was a young man, I worked as an attendant on a big-city ambulance. It was heartrending to pick up dead or dying people who woke up that morning with no idea it was their last day.

I saw many people on their final day on the planet: the beautiful Samoan man whose wife couldn't read the instructions on his medicine and had him drink it, rather than rub it on his arm. The family spread out on the highway after hitting a bridge abutment. The British tourist who looked the wrong way and stepped right in front of a speeding car.

They all thought this was going to be just another day on the planet. What might they have done differently if they knew this was the end? What would you do?

We are meant to play and laugh and love. Starting right now, live each moment as if it is your last.

One ambulance call above many sticks in my mind. We were called out in the early evening for an injured man. When we got to his home, we found a 24-year-old father of two with multiple stab wounds. "It is his birthday," I heard his wife say as I prepared him for transport to the hospital. She described how there was a disagreement about the music at his party and it had ended in her husband's stabbing. "Help him!" she said repeatedly as I rolled him to the ambulance.

We couldn't take her children in the ambulance so she went to find a ride to the hospital while we sped off into the night.

He was in bad shape.

Knife wounds don't appear as bad as other trauma — like gunshots or car crashes. Sometimes they aren't even bleeding.

These looked like clean incisions. Under the skin was the real damage. In an ambulance, there is no way to stop the internal bleeding that so many wounds can cause.

I counted eight wounds before I stopped counting and just talked with him. He was telling me, in a commanding and pleading voice, "Don't let me die!" I held his hand and lied to him.

The driver had radioed ahead and a trauma team was waiting as we got to the hospital. I was still talking with him when we arrived, but he had stopped talking to me. The trauma team pushed him into the ER and went to work. We had to wait outside the treatment room until someone pushed our gurney back out. When it did come out, the nurse indicated he had died.

I felt the loss. I hadn't known him long, but I had been the last person he talked to on this planet. In his pain and fear I felt that I had seen something of the real person and I liked him.

As we got out to the corridor that led to our ambulance I spotted his wife and kids and other relatives.

She asked me if he was ok.

It was not my job to say anything about a patient's condition to anyone. I was told to refer any questions to the doctor or hospital administration.

I was certainly not the one to tell a woman her husband was dead. But I could not hide the look on my face.

She sank to the floor and let out a sound I have never heard before or since. An animal shriek of unbearable pain and loss. It shattered me and it silenced everyone in the corridor. I wanted to stop and try to console her.

My more experienced driver tugged on the gurney and indicated we should be out of there. I looked back as we went out the swinging doors and saw her family holding her.

I never saw her again.

But I did see her husband. The firm I worked for had a number of contracts for the city, and one of them was the coroner's contract. Whenever a body needed to be transported, our firm was called. It was just coincidence that later that night my ambulance was called to move his body from the hospital to the morgue. The police and coroner had done their preliminary work and my job, once we got to the morgue, was to strip him, wash him, weigh him, measure him, and put a tag on his toe.

Then I put him on a tray that slid into a large cooler.

Afterward, I stepped outside to get some fresh air in my nostrils and was taken at how beautiful and sweet the night was. I was alive.

I was alive! For a brief moment, I had a glimpse of what that meant. I was only 18, but I was alive. I thought of the dead man whom I had only known a short while but who would be with me for a lifetime, and I vowed I would never waste my time on stupid, meaningless things.

I would never forget that life is temporary and so fragile. I would live my life fully. I never got to thank him.

But that man, in his dying, gave me a gift that would never leave me.

It's so easy to lose yourself in a poor definition of a life well lived — of time well spent — and also lose clarity on what it means to be human. We sometimes think a good life means accomplishment or money, and it really doesn't mean either.

We are meant to play and laugh and love. It is our birthright to be a part of the naturally unfolding mystery of life.

People who think they have it all figured out are often surprised at the end of their life that all they thought mattered so much doesn't really matter much at all.

Starting right now live each moment as if it is your last.

You won't remember to do it all the time. None of us does. But even if it's only echoes in the background, you'll have an ongoing reminder of how you should live and what you should say yes or no to.

When you think about stepping out and speaking up, when you think about doing something totally unexpected and slightly dangerous — something "wrong" — consider what you would do if you really lived as if life were finite. What is important to you when you know your time is limited? If you knew your time were up soon, would you care about things like what music was playing at your birthday party?

CHAPTER 3

It Isn't Safe to Play It Safe

Michele finished the "I want" exercise — designed to uncover what each person really wants — and without looking at anyone she rushed out of the room, got in her car, and drove away. She didn't tell me why until a year later, long after the leadership program she was in was over.

She called me at home then to tell me what had happened.

"On that day, I was looking over what I had written, and I was suddenly reminded of how important music was to me. All through my childhood I had wanted to be a clarinet player in a symphony orchestra. I worked hard and was sure this was going to happen for me. I could actually *see* myself onstage with the orchestra.

"One day my parents sat me down and had a hard talk about how few musicians actually make a living and that I should put aside my music and focus on something practical like accounting. It didn't happen right away, but I slowly turned away from my childhood dream and went on to get a degree in accounting.

When we try to play by the rules, we often find we've given up our dreams in exchange for an income.

"My parents were right. It was much easier to get a job with that degree than it would have been with a clarinet." (Her job was leading the accounts payable team at a hospital — collecting money people didn't have.) "But on that day in the workshop, the loss I felt in not following my dream hit me hard. I went home and sat on the floor outside the closet where my clarinet was stored and I cried. I hadn't played in years. I got it out of the closet and tried to play. I sounded awful, which was probably a combination of my rustiness and the clarinet needing a tuneup.

"I got the tuneup and starting taking lessons again. My skill returned very quickly. And when I saw an advertisement for an opening at the local symphony, I auditioned. I got the job and I'm calling to invite you to the Christmas concert where I have a solo."

Michele changed her life completely without quitting her job. The old dream of being in a world-famous orchestra had evolved, and this new dream made her happy.

Some childhood dreams simply age away. Maybe they came from a passing love of a fictional character or an impression from someone we admired.

But some dreams come directly from the heart. They have a power that feels like the dream is meant to be — like you were born to live this thing. Going against a dream like this takes lifetime effort and hurts the soul. Eventually, you die full of regrets. But as long as you are still alive you can come back to the dream.

Maybe you always wanted to be a ballet dancer. You got older, got a serious job and let the dream go. You have to push hard to keep it away. You don't even go to ballet performances anymore because it's just too painful.

But on some days, when you close your eyes you see yourself gracefully moving across the floor, your body expressing something you can't say in words.

If this happens to you and your youthful dream won't die, then you have to honor it. You don't have to upend your life, quit your job, and take lessons full time until you are dancing with the Bolshoi. All you need to do is start. Start taking lessons. Go see some ballet. Enjoy some videos of outstanding dancers. The connection will feed your soul in surprising ways. And even if the Royal Ballet isn't knocking on your door, other things could change.

Along with her music, Michele discovered the life she was living wasn't very fulfilling. She moved jobs from accounts payable to recruitment. She now enjoys her days matching professionals with the place she loves to work. And a big part of her life is her joy in playing with a symphony, as she always dreamed she would. The look on her face is one of contentment.

It wasn't easy for her to change, but it was much easier than living her life with a constant longing and regret.

When we try to play by the rules, we often find we've given up our dreams in exchange for an income.

CHAPTER 4

Are You Living Someone Else's Life?

We have one shot at this life. Bonnie Ware, a nurse in Australia, wrote in her blog of the top wishes of the dying: "I wish I'd had the courage to live a life true to myself, not the life others expected of me." By the time most of us have realized that, it's too late. Not too late for you, though. You're still breathing. Start right now.

You can choose to live in one of four different ways. Here they are from the worst to the best.

PRETEND TO BE SOMEONE ELSE AND FAIL. This is what a lot of people do when they don't trust themselves. Live life using somebody else's ideas and approaches. Go against your own instinct and judgment. Do things you think are wrong or unethical. Do all this and still fail.

This may be the worst choice because, not only is your life a failure, you've had no joy and you can't even say you tried your best. You tried someone else's approach over your own objections and you failed. On the last day of your life, you would probably look back and call it pathetic.

Your life on earth means something to you and those around you. You've had a glorious ride.

PRETEND TO BE SOMEONE ELSE AND SUCCEED

You adopt someone's mannerisms, you shout at people the way others do, you work behind colleagues' backs (this is the best place to be if you plan to stab them), you huff and puff and it all works out. You are in the right place at the right time and it all goes your way.

But this is truly a nightmare. Now you have to pretend for your entire career. You've got to take your lies and bluster and your imitation success to your deathbed. You have to remember forever how to be someone else in order to succeed. It's exhausting and not very satisfying. Yes, you will have had a form of success, but it still wasn't you and what you wanted. You would have some small sense of success, but on that last day, when your one life is over, you would probably label it sad.

BE YOURSELF AND FAIL

You're honest with yourself and you make your own path. Of course you look at and learn from other people. You're often trying out new ways of doing things, but you temper it all with your own internal wisdom. This keeps you learning, and also true to yourself. You do all of this with enthusiasm and you still fail.

No matter what you do, it doesn't work out. But it was a good fight. You brought all of yourself to the arena and with the best of who you are, you still weren't enough.

It's ok. Sometimes the challenges are just too great.

Living life this way, you have the possibility of redefining success. You have given life a genuine try, and it didn't work out the way you wanted. Not everyone who strives wins the gold. But you were on the field. And in many important ways it feels good to have given life a genuine try. You can at least be at peace.

BE YOURSELF AND SUCCEED

You listen to yourself and others. You learn and accept help when it's needed. The challenges arrive and you rise to them, failing at some and winning at others. You learn enough from earlier failures to win the day when the same challenges show up later. You compromise when that's wise, cooperate every chance you get, and fight when there is no other way to move forward. You never compromise your values, and your soul thrives. Your life on earth means something to you and those around you. In the end, we all die. It doesn't matter. You've had a glorious ride.

CHAPTER 5

No Time to Improve

The man I was coaching had a good heart. He also had excellent business skills. What he didn't have were people skills. Because of his inability to relate to people in a positive way, he had a hard time keeping staff, and the staff he did keep wasn't very happy.

When we did a quick co-worker assessment it was clear that people admired his ability to understand the challenges the business had, to recognize the competitive environment, and to hire the right people for the job.

What he didn't do well was understand and deliver what people needed to be inspired and motivated. He was a perfectionist and engineering-minded, and he expected things to work the way they had been designed and agreed. But there were humans involved and this irritated him.

Not surprisingly, he had heard he was not as effective with people as he was with numbers many times before. He had taken classes, read the right books, and really tried. But everyone knew he was straining when he came out of his office to meet people. Plus, it made him sweaty

We have limited time. While it's good to be always learning and improving, we have to decide when we're wasting time on something that will never get much better.

and miserable. He preferred issuing orders and writing memos to asking for input and talking to people. He was, and is, a successful introvert.

But he did see what was going on. When I asked him to tell me about his people, their strengths and weaknesses, he was very accurate, as far as I could see. But when he engaged with people he would only talk about what was wrong or what was lacking. There was no encouragement or recognition of their contributions.

This was just him. It wasn't him trying to be nasty. It was the way he dealt with himself and his world. He wanted to know how he could change to be more personable. I told him to forget about it. It wouldn't work. At his age, he could certainly still change anything he wanted. But he had tried this before and it hadn't worked. Why did he think it was worth his time now?

He could spend a lot of time and money trying to change things he might never be able to change. I can understand wanting to get better at something. But I asked him to face the fact that some people who are awful at a particular task at 30 will likely be awful forever. I didn't want him to waste his time.

He had to do the basics of the job. As a manager, for example, he had to know planning, budgeting, staffing, and so on. But on that list of required skills there were some he did well and others that gave him trouble. With limited time and money available for him to improve, what should he focus on?

First, I asked him to list what he was world class at. That was so he could feel good. Then we listed what he failed at regularly. Those tasks were on a list to be delegated. Finally, we looked at what he did well that he could learn to do at a world-class level. He picked one from that list to focus on over the next year.

Since he was good at paying attention to other's skills, he settled on the solution of promoting one of his staff to a position he called chief of staff. This person did have people skills and had the ability to translate the boss's disappointment into constructive questions, meetings, and solutions.

The chief of staff solution worked wonders. The boss sometimes still put his foot in it, but the chief was there to smooth things over. The boss respected what the chief accomplished and tried to improve what he could.

He made some progress, but in the end gave more of what he was bad at over to the chief. Everyone came out ahead.

We have limited time. While it's good to be always learning and improving, we have to decide when we're wasting time on something that will never get much better.

CHAPTER 6

"You Are An Idiot!"

When the holidays came, all my fellow year-abroad students took off to see some of the other delights of Europe. I, being poor, stayed behind and read and pretended that I was sightseeing where I studied — Pisa. In fact, it was a good place to visit and I enjoyed a large part of my time alone. I read and wrote and visited corners of the town I hadn't seen before. But I was always alone. As Christmas got closer, I began to feel the enormity of spending that first Christmas totally away from family and friends.

On Christmas Day, it really hit me. When I was a kid, we used to have wonderful family meals at my grand-mother's house. Lots of food, laughter, meaningful discussion, and presents. This Christmas had none of those. Even the hotel restaurant had closed early.

I really got deep into feeling sorry for myself. How would I make it through the day without great food or presents? Life felt bleak. I couldn't even afford to tele-phone home. And my favorite desk people from the hotel were gone to celebrate with their own families. Then I had an idea.

Not even a lonely, hungry, and homeless man with no legs would eat with me.

There was a shop that cooked chickens, vegetables, and roasted potatoes about a 15-minute walk from the hotel. I could go there, buy a feast and bring it back to the hotel and have my own meal.

It was dusk and a gentle rain was falling as I went out of the hotel and headed around the back. I had my head down against the rain as I came onto a large piazza. About halfway across, I heard someone shouting. At first, I paid no attention. I had quite a bit of Italian by then, but I was sulking in English and listening in on someone else's conversation still required translation. Finally I understood that a man was yelling at me to come closer to him.

When I got closer, he shouted at me, "What's the matter with you. Why are you all sad?"

I suppose something in my walk gave that away. I told him about my first Christmas away from home with all my friends gone and how I was lonely and sad.

"You're an idiot!," he shouted at me.

I was surprised at his lack of compassion. Maybe a little irritated.

"Why am I an idiot?"

"Look at me....*look*!"

And for the first time, I looked at him.

He saw that I saw him and started reprimanding me. I didn't understand every word he said, but I got his meaning.

"It's Christmas and I'm out here by myself in the rain with not even a hotel room to go to. I have no family, no food and no legs. And you whine and moan about how unfortunate you are. You're an idiot!"

I was shocked that I could have missed such an important fact about the man I was talking to. I suppose I thought he was just sitting down. But the truth is I didn't look closely. He was on a small platform with wheels. He had two things that looked like leather toilet plungers that he used to push himself along.

I had an idea.

"How about if I go and get some food and we go back to my hotel to eat Christmas dinner?"

He looked at me with disgust.

"I wouldn't eat dinner with you if you were the last person on the planet. You are too depressing." And then he pushed off toward an alley near the edge of the piazza. I stood there dumbfounded, with my mouth open, until he was out of sight and I didn't hear the wheels on his cart any more.

This pretty much completed my day. Not even a lonely, hungry, and homeless man with no legs would eat with me.

Then a strange feeling came over me. I suppose I was down about as low as I could go so I couldn't feel worse. But suddenly the humor of my situation was clear and I began to laugh. I kept chuckling all the way to the shop. I bought my meal and a small bottle of wine and went back to my room and had my feast. It was a great holiday meal. I toasted my absent dinner partner and thanked him for showing me something important. I talked throughout the meal as if I were in the middle of a family. Then I read a book until I was tired and went to sleep.

I've tried, not always successfully, to truly see the people I'm talking with. Not every problem is as obvious as a double amputation, but everyone has something I should be aware of. So I try to look and listen more than talk. It might have been the most important lesson I learned in my year abroad.

CHAPTER 7

How to Survive a Crisis

When I lived in Alaska and wanted to learn to fly, I also decided it would be a good idea to take a survival course. I signed up at the local community college for a course with a man who taught wilderness survival to Special Forces. It was an evening course and it was full. Our teacher was average in height and build and had a great sense of humor. But he didn't start off funny.

"When there is an accident or crash locally and I'm invited to help, I go on two kinds of mission. The first is a rescue mission. I like those because I'm bringing home living people who will heal and go on to live their life.

"The second is recovery. This is where I'm bringing back bodies. What determines whether I'm bringing back a living person or a body? Of course, some events are not survivable — a plane crash into a cliff, an avalanche in a mountain valley. In some situations, it won't matter what you do. But in most it will.

"You might guess it would be training that separates the survivors from the dead. That's not been my experience. Some of the most highly trained people don't make

The true attitude of the survivor is a passion to do the next thing that needs to be done — *right now.*

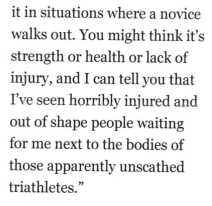

it in situations where a novice walks out. You might think it's strength or health or lack of injury, and I can tell you that I've seen horribly injured and out of shape people waiting for me next to the bodies of those apparently unscathed triathletes."

So what makes the difference?

It's attitude. And before you leap to a conclusion about what kind of attitude, I want to tell you it's not necessarily optimism. It's true that if you think all is lost you are unlikely to keep fighting. But the true attitude of the survivor of horrible circumstances is a passion to do the next thing that needs to be done — *right now.*

If you have just crashed your plane and you are hanging in the forest canopy upside down with a broken ankle and gasoline dripping on you, you don't have even one minute to think about why this happened to you or whether you have a good chance of getting out alive. You have to get yourself out of the fire hazard and onto the ground. Then, staying near enough to the plane to be found and far enough away so you won't be injured in the fire, you have to stabilize your injuries, find some shelter, and see what's next.

If you try something that doesn't work — you make a shelter from pine branches and it leaks horribly — you decide what to do next and you do it. Right away.

The instructor took us through a process of inventorying. He asked us all to empty our pockets, purses or backpacks onto the tables in front of us. For each item, we were to come up with 10 things that item could do in addition to its primary purpose. We were all amazed at the survival gear we had inadvertently brought with us.

Condoms, for example, can be used to keep your tinder dry, to start a fire (they burn hot for a few minutes), as the stretchy part of a slingshot, to carry water, as a clumsy rubber glove, as a fishing bobber, to hold a bandage in place around an extremity, and I'm sure you can think of more.

Tampons are incredibly useful in survival situations. They can be unrolled for a sterile wound dressing, used as a first filter to clean muddy water, are perfect as dry tinder for fire starting. The string can be used for all things string can be used for. The package can keep your matches dry and can be tied off with the string to use as a fishing bobber.

There were multiple examples of everything you'd find in a pocket or purse. But his real lesson was a broader one. When we are in survival mode we have to look at everything we have and determine how it can be used in other ways to meet the present emergency.

CHAPTER 8

Smile of the Old Man

When I was 18 I was faced with a decision I knew would affect the rest of my life. I was in college and I was so disappointed in what I was seeing. The classes weren't very challenging, the professors were mostly disengaged and distant. The biology course, for example, was taught by the professor in lecture form to a large hall. We couldn't ask questions — we had to save those for the lab days. Labs were led by grad students who were only doing it for the miserable salary. I could learn as much by just reading the book. I thought I had made a terrible mistake by coming to college.

But one teacher was marvelous. She was in her first year teaching freshman English and she was excited about the possibilities. The first task she gave us was reading *Death of a Salesman* and determining if Willy Loman's life was tragic or pathetic. This assignment really got my interest.

My assessment of success along the path in front of me was that it would be fairly easy to succeed. The barriers were not that high and I could see that by simply putting my hand on the shoulder of the person in front

I knew instantly that I would rather die with a smile on my face than suffer that last hour full of regret and sadness.

of me I could get my degree, find a good job, and build a career. But is that what I wanted? I didn't want to end up as the person who worked for 40 years and who suddenly realized he had lived a life he didn't want to live. I thought my deathbed realization would be that my life had been pathetic.

On the other hand, if I struck out in a direction of my own, with a plan to live on my own terms, when I reached my final hours I could be satisfied, even if it all went wrong, that I had lived a life worth living and could die in peace.

So I had to decide if I was going to stay in school and leave with a degree or leave now and take my chances. A degree would open many doors. I knew that then.

Without a degree I'd have to scramble and improvise. I wasn't sure that was the road I wanted.

I tried to decide. I made lists and tried to prioritize them. No clear decision emerged. I talked to friends and asked their advice. It was mixed and didn't help me decide.

I went to an empty room in my dorm. The furniture was there, but the mattresses were gone. I lay down on the bare springs and looked at the ceiling. I had begun to despair that I wouldn't figure out what to do.

Suddenly I experienced a leap in time. I was transported to the last hour of my life. I was old and in a clean bed. I was on the second floor of a house and it was springtime. The window was open and I could smell the spring and hear children playing outside.

I was alone but didn't feel lonely. In fact, I felt free of all expectations. Nobody was with me, so what I did next was not influenced by my parents, my spouse, my children, or any societal expectation of what was right or wrong.

In that solitude where I knew the end was near I began going over my life. I went to various events as I played back my time on earth from the end working back to the beginning. Most were kind of gray since I hadn't lived them yet. Then I got back to this moment of me lying on those steel springs. I played out the two rough directions I had identified — stay with college or head out into the unknown.

And that's when it became clear. From a perspective of my last hour one choice brought tears of sadness to the old man's eyes. The other path brought a smile to the old man's face. I knew instantly that I would rather die with a smile on my face than suffer that last hour full of regret and sadness.

I withdrew from school, took what little money I had to buy a one-way ticket to Hawaii (as far as I could go without a passport and warm enough if I had to live on the streets), and took off to find a different life. It hasn't always been easy, but it turned out to be the right thing to do.

There haven't been many conscious crossroads with such importance in my life. But whenever I take myself back to my last hour and ask if it will make the old man smile, I have always been able to decide.

The truly important things in life should be decided from the perspective of a life, not from a friendship, a marriage, or a career. It's the only perspective that holds up until the final hour.

CHAPTER 9

Don't Hit the Tree!

I was with a driving instructor who was showing me how to survive on slippery, dangerous roads. On the practice course were small cones that outlined the road and larger ones that represented trees. He had me going faster and faster around the curves until I was at the edge of my ability. As we came into one sharp turn, he shouted to me, "Don't hit the tree!" I promptly skidded off the "road" and flattened the cone that represented the tree.

"Do you know why you hit that tree?" he asked. I told him I was going too fast and lost control. He said that wasn't it at all.

"The moment I shouted to you to avoid the tree, that's all you focused on. So of course, you ran right into it. If you want to avoid the trees, focus on the road where the trees aren't. *Look at where you want to go, not at what you don't want to hit.*"

CHAPTER 10

I Just Don't Have the Time

A friend and colleague discovered one day she had inoperable cancer. She was told she had about two years to live. After the initial shock and letting friends and family know how much they meant to her, she went back to work. She didn't tell her co-workers about her illness, but something was different about her.

She was more open with people and a little more generous. Even though her firm was fairly competitive, she stopped competing and just enjoyed her work. But here is the biggest change: She stopped doing anything she thought was in any way destructive or stupid or a waste of time. She just wouldn't do it.

She wasn't nasty about it. Sometimes we are asked by someone with more power to do something stupid. And it's quite possible that something that was truly useful in some way just didn't look useful to her. In any case, when asked to do something she didn't want to spend her precious time on, she simply said, "I'm sorry, I just don't have the time."

She said it in such a way, with confidence, cheer and finality, that people seldom pushed back. If they did

What would you *do* if you knew you had only one hour to live?

she would listen intently and repeat that she really didn't have the time.

It turned out she didn't have two years, she only had one.

Time might be infinite and have no beginning or end. It might be possible to slow time or change the past. I don't know. Whatever we know about time, we know that our time on this planet is finite and short.

The hell of it is we have no idea how short. We all know intellectually that we'll die, but we all pretend we won't. Or we pretend it will happen so far in the future as to be meaningless.

My experiences as an ambulance attendant made me acutely aware of our fragility. Not one dead accident victim thought when they woke up that morning that it was their last day.

Think about it. What would you do if you knew you had only one hour to live? Who would you call? Who would you hug? What experiences would you seek out in that final hour?

What if you had a day? Most people will do a more intense version of their last hour if they know they have only a day left.

What if you have a week left on the planet? How about a month?

One of my favorite discussions about this final month involved things on the bucket list. One young woman said that she would go skydiving, but only on day 30 in case she had a fatal accident on the jump. She didn't want to lose her remaining time by dying on the first day.

Another woman spoke up in passionate disagreement. "I'm going skydiving on day one!" she said. "What if I really love it and I only try it on my last day. That would be the real waste."

These discussions got me considering what to do with my time. And got me wondering if there were any way to approximate how much time I have left. I developed something I called my "family death math." By looking at the death age of the men in my family, barring accident, I could approximate a likely minimum length of my life. The death age of all my male family members was right around 66. I'm a little over 64 today so if I round in my favor and do the math I have 730 days left on earth. If I'm more generous with myself and imagine that because of more healthy habits (most of my relatives smoked and drank, loved deep-fried food, and carried more weight than they needed) and imagine I'll live 20% longer, then I have about 5,500 days left. That puts me at 79. Not a bad age from where I sit at 64, although I can imagine it doesn't look so comforting from 78.

So if I figure I have years ahead of me, what will I do with my time? Certainly being aware of my mortality I try every day, sometimes successfully, to be grateful for all I have. I try, with the same level of success, to let those I love know how I feel. But I can't just hang around telling people I love them. I also want to work. I have ideas about how I can be useful and my ideas involve other people where they work. I want to meet them and hear them and help them do whatever great things they are attempting.

At the same, time I've become more comfortable just doing nothing. Nothing ... as in walking on the beach or in the woods. Nothing ... as in reading or talking aimlessly with a friend. The only criterion is how I would feel if this were my last hour. If I would regret an action in my last hour, I should never do it at all.

I like to think we'd all stop doing useless and destructive things if we knew how short our time was. We really don't have the time.

CHAPTER 11

How to Shoot Yourself in the Foot

I was early into a project to spread a new way of working in a British hospital. We were trying to install an exciting and innovative team approach to replace a top-down method. The group I was working with had discovered a way of saving the hospital a substantial amount of money — about £60,000. They were very proud of their work and we talked about making a presentation to the CEO.

This presentation was important for a number of reasons. It would give the CEO a story to tell in her quest to lower unnecessary costs. It would let the team know their work was important enough to be noticed by the top person. It would also, by letting everyone know the CEO was watching and approving, energize the approach I was using for big change.

The CEO agreed to meet, and we put her visit on the calendar. The team was so excited they prepared as if the queen were arriving. They polished the floors, painted the areas of most obvious need, cleaned up clutter, and really got the place ready.

The CEO now represented the worst of management, and it was clear there was one side that was the hardworking staff and the other side — the enemy — made up of bureaucrats who don't see or don't notice or don't care when the staff really does the hard work to improve.

Then they put together their presentation and practiced it, including answering questions they thought the CEO might ask. They were ready. On the day of the presentation everyone looked their best. People came in to work who were not on shift just to be a part of the visit.

About 10 minutes before the CEO was due to arrive, her Executive Assistant called to say something had come up and she would not be visiting today.

The team took it very well. They were under no illusions that they were the most important thing in the CEO's calendar and they simply rescheduled.

The CEO scheduled and postponed two more times. By now the group was pretty sure they were getting a message: "You aren't that important, so stop wasting my time."

I met with the CEO again and asked if there were a way we could make this short visit a priority. I told her the presentation was only five minutes long, in recognition of her busy schedule. She could stay for questions if she wanted but everyone would recognize if she had to rush off. Only please don't blow off a fourth meeting. She agreed that whatever happened she would make the next meeting.

She was true to her word this time, although nobody actually believed she'd show up. They did clean, but they didn't polish. And nobody came in unless they were getting paid.

The team sat around a rectangular table from the lunch room with the CEO at the head. They did a great job of showing how they had discovered the problem, what they implemented to keep it from happening again, and how much money they saved. The CEO listened with what we all thought was a slight smile of approval on her face.

When the team concluded the presentation, the CEO closed her notebook and gathered her things to get ready to leave. As she stood up she said, "I just have one question for you." Everyone was mentally going over the questions they had rehearsed. But they hadn't rehearsed this one.

"Why did it take you so long to find this problem?" And she left.

People who lead like that think they are being direct and honest. They think these are the questions that people who have had a success should be asking. And maybe she worked that way herself. But the true effects of her comments were all negative.

They were too polite to call her names in front of me, but I did hear of some conversations after. The CEO had not made a single friend or ally that morning. When she would later have staff meetings or send out messages of improvement, everyone dismissed them as not being worthwhile. She now represented the worst of management, and it was clear there was one side that was the hardworking staff and the other side — the enemy — made up of bureaucrats who don't see or don't notice or don't care when the staff really does the hard work to improve. Why bother?

When I think of all the things she could have said in those moments that would have changed the trajectory of that place, I'm both baffled and saddened. She could have said, "Thank you for all your hard work. You've done a good thing here." That would have been enough.

She could have said, "This presentation is very exciting and I'd like others to hear it. Would you be willing to make this presentation to others?" That way she could hope to duplicate their success more quickly in other departments.

But what she said was a dismissal and an insult.

I worked with her for most of a year after that. She often wondered why she wasn't getting more energy and enthusiasm behind her initiatives. We all tried to tell her, but we never made any progress.

She never even noticed she walked with a limp.

CHAPTER 12

Do You Know Why?

I was leading a workshop of 24 people. It was common practice in this hospital to share the attendee list a week before the program. As soon as the list was circulated, my phone started ringing with people who wanted to cancel.

The problem was one man who was in charge of safety for the hospital. People who had dealt with him wanted nothing to do with him and certainly didn't want to spend three days in close contact with him. He was described as cold and uncompromising. He had made a lot of lives miserable with his unwillingness to compromise on almost any safety problem. If it was a problem or a danger, he insisted it be fixed before anything else was done. Nobody liked to see him coming down the hall.

I replaced a few people on that course, but most decided they would give it a try after I told them that maybe they would know a little bit more about him and why he acted the way he did after the course.

People were polite but wary with him for most of the three days we worked together. He himself was

She was put on oxygen — or so they thought. A key valve was closed so no oxygen was delivered. Her brain died and by morning her body gave up and his wife was gone. All for an earache.

obviously introspective and reserved.

On the last day of the course, there was an opportunity to speak about issues close to your heart. It was billed as speaking your personal vision and was always an emotional event. It offered people a chance to get a small glimpse into what their colleagues seldom would speak about at work — what excites and motivates them.

When this man stood up to share, a large number of people thought they knew what they would hear. I had heard them talk about how he was motivated by details, by procedures, by processes. That's not what they heard at all.

"My wife and I were together for 22 years until the night she had an earache," he began. The pain in her ear got progressively worse until they decided they needed to go to the emergency room. While she was being evaluated, someone gave her a large dose of a pain killer she was allergic to. This allergy information was available to the hospital, but it wasn't noticed in time. She went into shock and was given another injection to neutralize the pain killer. This would have been the right thing, except it was the wrong dose. Her heart stopped and was re-started. She didn't immediately regain consciousness. She was put on oxygen — or so they thought. A key valve was closed so no oxygen was delivered. Her brain died. By morning, her body gave up and his wife was gone. All for an earache.

He vowed on that morning, through tears and anger, that he would quit his current career in finance and go to work in medical safety so that no one ever had to go through what he went through that night. "And that," he told the group, "is why I sometimes seem so hard on you. I'm just trying to make it safer for people to bring their loved ones to the hospital."

In an instant, the image people had of this man changed. People left their seats with tears in their eyes to hug this human being who only moments before had occupied the space of despised bureaucrat.

His image and reputation changed dramatically from that day. And although the lesson that we don't know what motivates people might be obvious, there is another lesson. Unless you share what motivates you, people have to pretend they know. It took a lot of courage for this private man to share his sorrow, but it made him a far happier man and far more productive in his chosen work.

We just don't know what motivates people until we truly listen. Stop explaining the actions of other people when you truly know so little about them. Ask and listen instead.

CHAPTER 13

Choose Compromise Last

When most people hear the word "conflict" they imagine something negative. It could be war, fights, or simmering rage. Conflict can eventually become all those things, but in its purest form it's simply a differing point of view.

We often jump to compromise in a conflict. It seems like the right thing to do. You show good faith by offering some sacrifice and your opponent does the same thing. It looks like the way to end the conflict. But it's actually a recipe for disaster. You start off aiming for a lose/lose solution, which is the definition of compromise — I'll agree to lose something if you will. You might blunt the conflict this way, but working together afterward is difficult if you both realize you've lost too much to make it worth working together at all.

There is a general notion that life would be better if there were no conflict. Maybe. But conflict is a powerful force and can have powerful, positive outcomes. Look at it like you look at the wind. It's neither good nor bad on its own. You can ignore it if it's weak, harness it to produce energy or move ships, and shelter from it when it gets to a dangerous point.

> Many conflicts
> are solved
> the moment
> two people
> understand each
> other.

Conflict, like the wind, can work for you. And with skillful involvement you can keep it from becoming a destructive tornado. The task is to look at the conflict in front of you with clear eyes and decide how best to approach it, to harness it.

First, listen to the other party until you truly understand what they are saying. Almost everyone has the experience of listening to two people arguing and realizing that they actually agree, but are nevertheless fighting because they're not listening to each other. Many conflicts are solved the moment two people understand each other.

When people are in conflict it doesn't matter what is actually happening. What's important is what they *think* is happening. Again, listening to what the other person wants, what they are afraid of, what they hope will happen, is necessary before you can begin to solve any conflict.

After listening to the other person, act as if they will adopt your model of trying to understand. They might not, but I know of no pressure, no fast talking, no threat that will make them listen to you. The only thing I've seen that encourages others to listen is to listen first.

In a true conflict, people feel threatened. They might even feel under siege. Nobody does well in these conditions, so a part of your job in solving conflict is to reduce or remove the threat. By showing you understand their point of view, even if you don't agree with it, you lower the danger.

There are at least five ways to react to conflict. Your natural reaction to conflict is something that's probably tied to your childhood and your personality. You have a preferred way to deal with conflict, which is great if the conflict in front of you is best handled in that way. But the wide variety of conflicts means you need a wide variety of tools.

1. You can go for "I win and you lose." This approach puts competition as the first instinct.

2. You can aim for an "I lose and you lose" approach. This is known as compromise.

3. You can run and hide. By avoiding the conflict it might die on its own. Sometimes, by avoiding conflict, you are conceding the point.

4. You can view the other party's point more positively than yours and accommodate, at the expense of your position.

5. Or you can collaborate with the other party to find a solution that works for both of you that isn't immediately obvious. This is the "I win *and* you win" approach.

Aggressively competing with your opponent is usually a recipe for more conflict. In certain situations it makes sense to try to impose your solution. This turns, temporarily, into I win, you lose. Go for *your* solution when:

- It's an emergency and there is no time to discuss options

- You are the expert and know something they don't

- Your position is unpopular, but it's your job to make this decision

It's easy to get this one wrong. You have no time to listen, you're essentially telling people to be quiet, and you might have over-estimated the emergency and your knowledge of the problem and the solution. Have you ever seen people convinced they knew better than everyone? Were they always right?

Compromise can be useful in rare situations. Even in compromise, you should attempt to be creative and come to an agreement that both sides can happily support. Compromise is in order when:

- It actually is better for each party to have a part of what they are after

- You have worked hard and fell short on collaboration

- Something needs to happen and compromise won't be destructive

The need for immediate compromise is much rarer than people think. Spend some energy and some time to see if there is a win/win hidden in the details. And when you are sure you've selected the right approach to a conflict in front of you, stop, listen, and think again about what you can do to reach a solution you both want.

Avoiding a conflict can be strategically sound. Just move away from the heat. It's smart to remove yourself from conflict when:

- You or your opponent needs a chance to cool down

- You need to gather more information

- The conflict is too trivial to bother with

- Time will remove the conflict on its own

It doesn't pay to avoid a conflict when it will get worse without attention.

Accommodating another person's point of view is a viable approach to conflict. You simply switch sides and help them get their way. Note that this is not a lose for you. You use this when:

- The issue is not that important for you

- You are wrong

- Working on a solution is a waste of time

But accommodating before you state your position isn't a good solution because it means your ideas aren't heard.

Collaboration means sitting down with your opponent in the conflict and working together to find a win/win. It requires a trust you might not feel and a willingness to show your hand that you might think is dangerous.

You should choose collaboration when:

- Teamwork is a desired outcome of the conflict

- The issue is too important for either party to lose anything

- You truly need a creative solution

Don't use collaboration on trivial problems. It takes too much time. In an emergency, you probably don't have time to use collaboration as a first response, but you might want to return to it after the fire is out.

Understanding the options you have for dealing with conflict is an important step in avoiding losing something or everything each time there is conflict.

CHAPTER 14

Halfway Doesn't Work

There's a common saying people like to use, especially when they are in conflict: "I'm willing to meet you half way."

Don't bother. If you go only halfway, you have no relationship, unless you consider head butting to be a relationship.

Imagine you are on one side of the room and the person you need to work with is on the other. If you come halfway across the room and they do the same, you are essentially nose-to-nose. You didn't move into their territory. You're not seeing the world from their point of view. You've only come a safe distance where you can wait for them to come further. As a sign of commitment to improvement, it's weak and ineffective.

If you go 60% of the distance to the other wall, you now have a 10% overlap. If they do the same, you have 20%. That works both in business and in relationships. Each of you has to do *more than half* to make it work.

The larger that overlap is, the greater the chance for a successful relationship.

It looks like this:

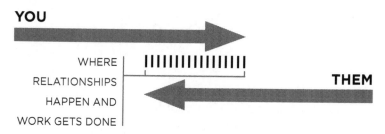

YOU

WHERE
RELATIONSHIPS
HAPPEN AND
WORK GETS DONE

THEM

This doesn't mean you become a doormat and go all out just to prove you can do all the work. And if it looks like that's happening, it may make sense to withdraw. But in a non-functioning relationship, someone has to start by proving their commitment to success. If you each wait and no one makes that statement of commitment, there is very little hope.

Don't meet anyone half way. Meet them as far as you can on their side. If you truly want to move forward, then commit to going beyond halfway as an investment in the relationship. Going only halfway is you waiting for them to prove they are committed before you commit. Show them first, commit, and go beyond.

CHAPTER 15

Skeptics Are Your Friends

I was working at a hospital and part of my job was to help various areas become more effective and efficient. I was an outsider with little medical experience, the hospital was in England and I'm American, and I was hired and introduced by the hospital administration. Three serious strikes against me.

During my introductory weeks, I attended a presentation by a management consultant who had been touring Emergency Departments around the country. She was good at her job and was helping many hospitals make good improvements. The CEO, COO, medical director, and other top people in administration were there. Many doctors had been invited.

The consultant introduced herself and began showing some of her slides with her conclusions. As she was speaking, one of the doctors raised his hand and was recognized. "Who are you?" he asked. She cautiously said that she thought she had introduced herself, and then began to do it again. He interrupted her with some passion in his voice. "No, I don't mean your name. I mean who are you to be presenting guesses about my

The way to diminish general pushback or eliminate it altogether is to embrace your skeptics.

Emergency Department. I've never even seen you there."

She began to explain how often she had been there. She even tried to apologize that they hadn't met.

"Look. I work a lot of shifts. I've been there over two decades and since we haven't met, you haven't been there nearly enough to even begin telling us what's wrong. I'm not going to listen to this." And he stormed out.

I looked over to the CEO and COO and they were both shaking their heads and then looking back toward the speaker. After the presentation was over, I asked about the person who had left. Every person in administration dismissed him as a trouble maker who just didn't like anything admin did. They all told me to stay away from him. He had nothing to contribute.

The nurses told a different story. They described him as an excellent doctor and a great human being. They told me admin didn't like him and they treated him poorly.

I made an appointment to meet with him.

We met at the ED during his shift. He was just leaving a patient and he saw me and pulled me into a small room. He began a 30-minute harangue that ranged over the years and all the ways he and his department had been mistreated. He told me where the administration and the government had got things wrong and what they needed to do to fix it. I had my notebook out taking notes the entire time. When he finished I looked at him.

"Now I get it." I said.

"What do you get?"

"I've been told that you are someone who hates management. I see that isn't true at all. What you hate is *crap* management."

He smiled and then challenged me. "Just what do you think you can do here?"

I asked him what was the thing that frustrated him the most. Was there something they knew was wrong but hadn't been able to fix? He said the worst problem was the backup that occurred in the ED waiting room when a major trauma came in. Everyone worked on the trauma, an auto accident for example, and all the normal traffic just sat there waiting.

I told him I had no idea if I could help, but I was willing to try. I asked him if he could join me sometime to watch a busy shift and actually *see* what happens during these events. Our job would be to just stay in one spot and look at what was happening. We wouldn't intervene. We wouldn't even speak.

About a week later, we stood in the ED watching the standard flow of injured, sick, and drunk people being treated. Then ambulances pulled up with the horribly injured victims of an auto accident, and the ED did what it's really good at doing: They orchestrated an incredible response to the mayhem and began saving lives.

As feared, the normal flow stopped. But it wasn't for the assumed reason. Yes, everyone was gathered around the accident victims, but most of them weren't working. They were watching. And they were watching because the senior doctor, the one who normally decided who worked on what, was working the trauma. He couldn't keep the schedule going and save lives at the same time.

The solution to the staffing problem was to have someone always prepared to take over scheduling duties as soon as the senior doctor was unavailable. Sometimes that would be a nurse, sometimes a doctor. They simply agreed at the beginning of the shift who was best prepared to match the skills of the staff with the needs of the patient.

Now I hadn't really done much. We'd used a simple tool and discovered an easy answer. But he was impressed and he opened his ED to me. He told everyone I was one of the good guys and that they should see if they could help me. That senior skeptic's endorsement didn't just make my work easier, it made it possible.

When you make a decision or lead a change, there will always be doubts and pushback. It's human nature. There is a good chance even *you* will have some doubts with the tougher decisions. The way to diminish general pushback or eliminate it altogether is to embrace your skeptics.

Be sure to differentiate between skeptics and cynics. Cynics don't like much of anything. They are critical for the sake of making life miserable. Typically, they are miserable in their own lives and just like to make certain everyone around them feels just as bad. "When a cynic smells flowers, he looks for the funeral."

Skeptics are thoughtful, experienced people. They have seen a lot of nonsense in their careers, and they know that many initiatives start but never finish. They've heard managers present ideas that had no chance of success. They've watched good ideas die because the person who introduced them failed to gain support and failed to act.

A skeptic is interested in success and willing to participate, but needs to know it's worth their time. Meet with key skeptics to enlist them as supporters.

And here's the magic. Thoughtful skeptics are widely admired in any organization. People often seek them out for advice because they know the skeptic will have looked at all angles. They are valuable because they don't have stars in their eyes. They see clearly and they don't mind saying what they see. So when you have the skeptics on board, you generally have everyone else, too.

Here are a few steps to help you enlist skeptics.

1. Think about what you want to accomplish and how you would describe it to a skeptic. Get it down clearly and succinctly before you take your message to them. Don't practice on skeptics. It never goes well.

2. Identify a key skeptic. You just have to ask people who they seek out for advice. These people are often, but not always, skeptics.

3. Present your idea to the skeptic as a draft, not a finished product. I know, you've worked as if it were final. But that was simply to make your own thinking clear. Talking to the skeptic should add to and expand your thinking. Ask for their advice, listen, and take notes.

4. Ask the skeptic who else you should talk to. Meet with those people under the same circumstances. Listen, take notes, and ask for advice.

5. Create a relationship map that shows where the skeptics are and who they interact with. If you ever want

to communicate with a larger group and can't meet with all of them, then just meet with the skeptics at the center of communication networks. They'll pass it on.

6. Keep the skeptics on your meeting list during roll out. Ask them to lunch and ask them to tell you what's working and what's not. The honesty of the skeptics is extremely valuable to you.

7. Give the cynics a little bit of time, but not too much. You do this only because you want to be certain they are cynics and not skeptics. Once it's clear the cynics can't be a part of what you're building, you have to move them out.

You don't have to be certain of what you will accomplish. You must have a clear goal, some idea of what you will need to get there, and a genuine willingness to listen to criticism and critical thinking. The input of skeptics makes any change so much easier.

We have a natural human tendency to seek out people who agree with us. It's a comfortable habit that seems to save us from conflict. But the people who are skeptical of what we're doing actually help improve our solutions. Skeptics have the added value of being leaders. If the key skeptic says it's good, then it must be good.

CHAPTER 16

Do You Have Any Facts?

I was doing a workshop that included eight surgeons. Surgeons, as you might have experienced, are very sure of themselves. Frankly, I wouldn't have it any other way. I mean, do you want your surgeon to be wishy washy? Do you want your surgeon to seek consensus at each decision point? "I don't know. What do you think? Cut here or a little farther down?" That's not a conversation you want to hear, even under anesthesia.

I like it when people who have difficult jobs are able to learn their job and then do it with confidence. Still, some people take it too far. They don't listen to anyone, they make mistakes they don't acknowledge, and they are sometimes accused of being egotistical.

My workshop was designed to help those in medical leadership roles get a better result when they had to work with others. I was speaking quite passionately about the importance of focusing on characteristics of group work that are difficult or impossible to measure, things like compassion, empathy and love, when I was interrupted by an eye surgeon.

Nothing that I really cared about could be measured. Nothing.

"Look, we as physicians have to practice evidence-based medicine. We need proof for what we say and do. You talk about all this love, compassion, empathy and other soft stuff — where is your proof ?"

I had to tell him it was a good question and I didn't have a good answer. He agreed to let me sleep on it and answer him the next morning.

I spent the evening thinking about what he said and worrying about how I would answer. I couldn't get to sleep. And then I had a blindingly obvious insight. Nothing I really cared about could be measured. Nothing.

Of course I was interested in having enough money to pay the rent and buy food. That could be measured. But if I had to choose between money and the love of my family, there would be no contest.

I thought about what friendship means to me and realized I couldn't use a number to rank its importance. I thought about how much I love my wife and realized there was no useful scale to measure that love. I considered the happiness and inspiration that art, music, and poetry had brought me and, again, I saw no way to quantify it.

The next morning I told him and the rest of the group about my failure to find any way to measure what I spoke about as important. I told them the things I spoke of as essential were only beliefs, but I held them powerfully.

They listened silently, then the surgeon who had asked the question agreed we could go forward on those terms.

CHAPTER 17

Negotiate So The Other Person Wins

I was bidding on some leadership work for a government agency, a part of the National Health Service, in the U.K. It was a long process that involved submissions to the European Union, advertising all over Europe and waiting. Lots of waiting. Finally, it was announced that I got the work. I was excited since it meant doing some of my favorite work and leadership workshops. A few days after the announcement, I got a call from the CFO of the organization. I thought he was calling to congratulate me and get to know me.

He did congratulate me and then, very quickly, got to the point. "You're going to cut your prices in half. We don't have the money to pay what you bid, so if you want the work you can take 50 percent of what you bid. Take it or leave it."

From *Getting Past No* by William Ury I knew a few things.

1. Whenever anyone says "Take it or leave it," you have a good chance of starting a negotiation. That saying

Whenever anyone says "Take it or leave it," you have a good chance of starting a negotiation.

That saying gives away the fact that your opponent has nothing left.

gives away the fact that your opponent has nothing left. It's an attempt to steamroll you because they are not confident they could win on merit.

2. I needed to stall for my answer and get off the phone so I could calm myself and regroup.

3. I didn't know enough about this man to find a win-win, and I would need to do some research.

I told him I'd need to think about his offer and hung up. I made some calls to people I knew who might know him and found out a few facts.

He was part-time in his position and looking to make a name for himself as a conserver of the organization's funds.

He had a reputation as a take-no-prisoners dealer and negotiator.

He either got what he wanted or he made your life miserable.

Ok.

Good start. My job was to give him what he wanted and still get what I wanted.

I didn't assume the number he gave me was precisely what he wanted. Fifty percent off was an arbitrary number, I guessed. What he really wanted was visible evidence that he won some concession after the contract was awarded.

He wanted to be a finance hero.

I could give him that. I called him back and said I would sign up to finish our contract for the number of sessions at the agreed price and then do one program for him at no charge. *Free.* It was not 50% off — more like 15%. But it gave him what he needed for a presentation to senior management.

It let him do his job and make a name for himself. I kept my fee the same and did my work. This is important. I didn't want to give so much away, but I had to let him save face or nothing would have gone well. We both won.

The deal also gave me time. Anything could happen during the time. In this case, events moved in my favor.

Shortly after I finished the last paid workshop, the agency was combined with another, the finance director left and the new organization was not ready to think about leadership training.

With no one to deliver the free workshop to, I offered the free workshop to the former CEO in his new post. This provided me a way to keep my word, thank him for his support, and meet some new people.

CHAPTER 18

How to Speak Like a Leader

The vision exercise in Chapter 12 really brings out the best in people. We are seldom invited to speak about what we truly want. At one event we were introduced to a leader who sat quietly among us.

After introducing the exercise, I opened the floor to whoever wanted to speak first. This first person is often someone who has been vocally involved in most of the events of the past days. But today's volunteer was the opposite. She was a quiet nurse who hadn't really said much of anything.

She was small physically and her voice was quiet, almost apologetic, at first. I leaned in to listen. She was in charge of the pediatric ward at this large organization. And she had a dream to turn that ward into a separate hospital. She envisioned a hospital within a hospital with different policies that recognized that children were not just smaller adults but were a special class all their own.

She spoke clearly about how some of the hospital operations short changed children, and yes, she understood how things had to be done uniformly to avoid

When she finished, many were in tears and everyone was emotional. I had to call a short recovery break.

chaos, but no, that did not mean rolling over the needs of our most vulnerable patients. Why, for example, did injured or ill children have to be pulled crying from the arms of their parents because of standard visiting hours? Why were adult doses of medicine even allowed on the ward?

She outlined the steps that would be needed and described the other changes she would make. She told the stories of a few children who had been harmed by business as usual and then described how they would be served by the new hospital.

We were all lucky to be there that morning to hear her speak. She showed us all what it means to lead. She had no orator's voice. We had to pay attention to hear her. But her passion was so great that her lack of volume and even lack of eloquence meant nothing. We all were certain we were hearing someone who would give everything for this cause. We knew she had thought about it thoroughly and we knew, because she told us, that there was a place in this campaign for everyone in the room. With her stories of vulnerable children fresh in the room, she asked us to consider how we wanted to treat our children, our future, and whether we were willing to stand up and do what needed to be done.

The thing that struck me that morning was, although the energy and involvement of the group built with each moment of her talk, she never seemed to raise her voice or really change the tone of her speech at all. She was so committed and passionate she didn't need to. We could hear the urgency in her quiet belief that changing how the hospital treated children was essential. We felt we knew the children who had been harmed. We felt we knew her, we knew there was no way she could fail, and we trusted her completely. Even though most of us had nothing to do with the present situation, we felt responsible now for the solution.

When she finished many were in tears and everyone was emotional. I had to call a short recovery break. A group of people swarmed the nurse with ideas and offers of help. The rest got coffee and sat to consider what this presentation meant for their own visions and what it meant for their lives.

I wandered around the room to make myself available for anyone who might need to talk and passed by the CEO and an eye surgeon. The surgeon was saying, "Now I know what's wrong with this place." The CEO, who had heard something along these lines from him before, warily asked him to continue. "You and I think we are in charge here, and *she* should be."

When you look around in daily life you notice that most people don't speak the truth. They don't say anything meaningful that truly touches you. This young woman hadn't spent hours rehearsing to get just the right words, she paid no attention to her body language or props. She simply spoke honestly about something that meant a lot to her. And her sincerity and passion were unmistakable. Everyone in that room wanted to help her reach her goal because of the way she had connected with them. Honestly, quietly, and without artistry. She touched something inside each of us with her stories.

That's how a leader speaks.

CHAPTER 19

Follow Your Leader Over a Cliff

After Ernest Shackleton and his crew were marooned when ice crushed his ship, he decided to take five men with him in one of the lifeboats and travel 800 miles from Antarctica to a whaling station on Elephant Island. It's one of the most amazing feats of seamanship ever. Fearing the wind and currents on the west side of the island would blow them right past the station, they landed on the opposite side of the island, 22 miles and one mountain range away from their destination. Two of the men were too ill to climb, and Shackleton left them with another man to watch over them. Shackleton and seamen Tom Crean and Frank Worsley set out to cross the range and get to the station.

They didn't have much to begin with, but they took no materials for tents or sleeping. They intended to march straight up and over and arrive without stopping. They had many setbacks as they started up promising slopes and found a sheer cliff on the other side. Exhausted, they finally reached a passable peak near sunset. The temperature was dropping and they could see a storm coming. All they could see of the slope they had to go down was snow disappearing into fog. What Shackleton

He had no time and no data to make a perfect plan. They had to do something and this was the only thing that would work — if it worked.

did then demonstrated why he was such as outstanding leader.

He said, "Boys, we're going to have to slide down. We can't go back and we can't stay here. The storm and the cold will kill us."

Crean and Worsley argued that this was extremely dangerous since they didn't know if the slope continued to the bottom or shot off a cliff.

Shackleton agreed. "We don't know how this will work out, but we know what happens if we stay here."

They continued to argue and Shackleton asked them for their alternate plans. Hearing none he said, "We have to get down now. If we stay here, we die." Then they sat down in single file, grabbed on to each other to form a human toboggan and started to slide. Worsley said that his hair stood on end and he became aware of a strange sound. It was very high-pitched and annoying. It took a moment, but then he realized he was making the sound. He was screaming. They were swallowed by the fog as they slid down the mountain. Then they were safely at the bottom and laughing. They were still far from their goal, but they had handled the worst of the climbing. And they were alive.

The genius of Shackleton was, normally, his planning. He was meticulous in all planning and preparation. He thought things through to make sure they were going to work, then he would decide and act. In this case, he had no time and no data to make a perfect plan. Sitting still meant they would die. And if they died, so would all the other members of the expedition. They had to do something and this was the only thing that would work, if it worked.

Risk is sometimes the only option in a world of unknowns.

I was working with a group of about 300 middle managers from a health insurance organization. Their company was losing money and they were in the middle of a major shakeup. Nobody knew who in the room would have jobs in a week or in six months. My job was to help get them ready for whatever was going to happen. The company wanted them to be optimistic, innovative, and capable if they were let go. They wanted the same if they stayed. We spoke about what they might do differently on Monday morning, and we were discussing some actions when a large part of the room erupted in disagreement.

"We can't do things like that! If we fail, we'll be fired."

I asked if that actually happened in their company or if it was a myth. Many people were convinced it actually happened so I offered the challenge. "Tell me the story of an individual who took a calculated risk, failed, and then was fired." I waited for about three minutes and nobody told me a story.

Then I asked them to think about the people who were moving quickly up the ranks. "Tell me about their risk taking and their failures and successes."

I heard a few stories about people who had big ideas, convinced the right people to try their idea, tried, failed, and got promoted. What was going on? No stories about firing, but already a handful about promotions.

It seems that as leadership looks around and decides who they want to join their ranks, they value calculated risk-taking over safety, comfort, and no new ideas. People who stood for something and were willing to risk failure were of more value than those who played it safe.

There is certainly room in your life to make big plans and to study those plans and their potential outcomes until you know the right course to take. Do that and make your calculated bets.

But also make room for big mistakes. There are times when you can't see the bottom of the hill, when you know you'd just rather lie down and go to sleep, but you also know doing that will mean the end. When you're faced with those challenges, why not risk it all? If you stay still, you're going to die anyway.

CHAPTER 20

Harvard Wins Over Texas

I was in Brussels to deliver a presentation to a group of global CEOs. There were about 30 people in the room and we were all listening to a professor from Harvard talk about his ideas for doing a better job with their business. I was half listening and half considering my own presentation when something happened that changed the room and changed the way I dealt with a specific problem for the rest of my career.

There were only about five American CEOs in the room of Europeans, and one of them led a Texas oil company. I'd talked with him at dinner the night before and he was smart and fast and direct in his speech.

The professor was talking about an approach that he was using in one of the firms he consulted for. He was a man who was putting his theories into practical use. Something he said struck the Texan as wrong and he just blurted out, "Bullshit!"

The professor stopped talking. Many heads turned to look briefly at that man who had breached European meeting etiquette in such a vulgar way. These were leaders who would not shy away from a disagreement or

"Many of my friends and respected colleagues hold the same position you do. But I cannot, and here is why..."

heated discussion. Far from it. But you just didn't shout "Bullshit!" in the middle of a presentation by a respected scholar.

I looked at him as he seemed to suddenly realize where he was and what he'd done. The look on his face was, "Did I really say that out loud?"

Now, as smart as the CEO was, the professor was smarter. He had more experience in varied industries, including oil, and had more facts and stories at the ready. In a battle of the wits, it would have been no contest. But the professor didn't fight back. He didn't become defensive. He simply said, in a tone of sincere invitation, "Tell me what you mean."

So many of us, when we're attacked, prepare for defense or attack. "You can't say that about my prized beliefs!" And so we ready for attack. We may win or lose the discussion, but either way somebody loses, and that isn't really what we want to have happen. Especially when we're presenting, we need to be humble and authoritative at the same time. We need to avoid being knocked down and we need to avoid knocking anyone else down.

The Texan hesitated and then began to describe his objection in more polite language. The professor listened and asked some clarification questions. When he was sure he understood the complaint, he turned and looked at the slide he was using when he made his statement. He looked at it for a long time. He looked at it like he had never seen it before. Then he turned around and said the few words that changed the course of the meeting.

"Many of my friends and respected colleagues hold the same position you do. But I cannot, and here is why..."

It was brilliant. In a few short words, he lifted the Texan up into the company of his friends and respected colleagues. He acknowledged that there could be reasonable views that conflicted with his. And he stood up for his own beliefs. The room was visibly relieved that a conflict had been avoided. The oilman recognized the gift given to him. I was moved by the generosity of the professor and also grateful for what he'd done to make the room easier to work with once I took the stage.

He showed how it was possible to avoid an either/or prison for differing ideas and allowed me to introduce some fairly radical ideas about compassion, trust, and love in the workplace. People felt free to question my assertions and I felt free to listen and respond without defense. It was a memorable day.

Today I try to emulate the professor. I hear even a vigorous disagreement as an opportunity to understand someone else, include them among my friends, and expand the conversation.

CHAPTER 21

Stand in Front of the Jet

A lot of dangerous activities happen on an aircraft carrier during launch and recovery of aircraft. There is one man on the ship who controls what goes on in that chaos, and it's not the captain and it's not the pilot. That man is called the deck boss. During launch, he tells the pilots exactly what to do, and they either do it or they don't fly.

Sometimes while launching aircraft there is a difficult moment when the pilot and the plane are attached to the catapult and engines are at full power, but the launch has to be scrubbed. Perhaps they have a problem with the catapult, or the ship is switching from launch to recovery. The pilot has to be ordered to shut down the engines, release the brakes and be disconnected from the catapult.

The pilot does not want to do this. In addition to the fact that every inch of the pilot is ready for launch, there is the problem that, if the catapult fires while the engines are shut down, the pilot will almost certainly be hurt. The lifeless plane will be flung in front of the huge, moving ship and there will be only a brief moment

If you want people to trust you, you have to be willing to put yourself at risk. You have to be vulnerable.

when they can bail out without hitting the ship. There are safeguards built into the system, of course, but no pilot wants to be slammed into the ocean. So they want to make sure they can trust the signals the deck boss gives.

What signal do you think the boss gives the pilot when he wants him to shut down the engines and disconnect? A lot of people choose the finger drawn across the throat as a sign to kill the engines. But that could also be interpreted as a sign "You're going to die" or "I'm going to kill you." No, the deck boss walks to the front of the plane, straddles the catapult and with his nose facing the nose of the plane, he crosses his arms across his chest. He's saying, "Shut down your engines. I am so convinced this is safe for you, I'm placing my life on the line to show that you can trust my signal." He stands there until the shutdown and disconnect are complete.

If you want people to trust you, you have to be willing to put yourself at risk. You have to be vulnerable. Too many employees are familiar with the manager who leads from way behind, takes credit for success, and finds someone to blame in failure. And sadly, that seems to be the model for too many mid- to senior-level people. In reality, you have to do it wrong. You have to lead from the front, give credit away for any success, and accept blame when there is a failure. If you can't do this, then you can't lead.

If you are the person who hires, trains, motivates, and supervises a group, then this makes perfect sense. You *are* responsible for failures. And if you're serious about motivation, you will recognize that a group whose manager or leader has their back is far more effective, innovative, and profitable than a group that is constantly looking over their shoulder to see if they'll be hurt by the person who is supposed to support them.

You have to earn trust. It's never given, it's never inherited. Mistrust is both given and inherited, and you may find yourself suffering unfairly for what the previous person in your job did. You may even be mistrusted based on the department you come from. It is unfair, but it's a fact. You always have to earn trust.

Earning trust is fairly straightforward, although it can take some time. The first thing to do is be honest. Every lie, no matter how big or small, is eventually found out. So always tell the truth. If someone asks you a question and you don't know the answer, just say so. If you can't answer because it would break a confidence, then say that.

Always do what you say you're going to do. Don't make promises you'll regret, but if you do promise, then make it happen.

Third, remember the deck boss and make yourself vulnerable. The leader who isn't out front, who has no skin in the game, or, worse, who blames the team when things go wrong, will never earn trust and will never be the leader of that team no matter where they are on the org chart.

If you want to earn trust, no matter how long you've been on the job, ask yourself "What do I have to *do* to earn their trust?" Then the answers and suggestions begin to flow.

1. I will go and listen to them. Find out where their frustrations and pains are.

2. I will make sure I understand, but I will make no promises yet.

3. I will take notes as I ask, "What do *you* think?"

4. I will make certain to meet with all the skeptics to hear what they have to say.

5. I will find as many things as I can that I will do right now to eliminate common problems. I will do them without fanfare or delay.

6. I will then meet with as many people as I can to talk to and lay out a path for accomplishing more complex things on the list.

7. I will make sure to talk about the things we can't tackle or can't yet tackle and explain why.

At this point the staff sees that you listen, they see a person of action instead of hollow words. You don't make promises you won't keep, you listen, and you care about the world they inhabit. You may not have earned trust yet — that can take some time — but at least you are seen as someone who doesn't deserve to inherit someone else's mistrust. It's a start.

CHAPTER 22

Small Tests of Change

I was consulting in a hospital when a doctor came to me with a problem. The neurological ward did most of the lumbar punctures (spinal taps) but they had no regular place to do them. When a patient needed one, they were put in any empty bed that could be found in this sprawling hospital. Once admitted, the doctor had to find them, do the procedure, get the samples to the lab, wait for results, consult the patient, and finally send a letter to the patient's doctor with the findings.

It wasn't working very well. Patients would arrive at the hospital only to be sent home again because there was no bed for them. Once the patient did find a bed, the doctor often couldn't find the patient. If they did find them, it was often late in the day and the lab day-shift would be closing soon. Off-hours work was more expensive and took longer. The patient and the doctor had to stay and wait for results or schedule another appointment. Missed connections, bad communication, expensive waits, and poor care were the result of this mess, and the doctor wanted to change it for the better.

He had some ideas about how to do that and had approached the manager of the ward. The manager said

All the questions and objections were already handled in the test. "What if..." questions that halt most new initiatives were already tested and answered.

no. "What we have now has worked for more years than I've been here. Let's not fool around with something we know works."

And in that last sentence is the key to working with bureaucracy. They need to know it works before they can give approval for testing. It sounds backward and impossible, but that's the way it works. So we went at it in a different way.

We planned a small test of change. We wanted to prove that a fixed place, fixed schedule, and early intake saved time and money and increased patient satisfaction and outcomes.

First, we measured what we had already. We counted the number of missed or cancelled appointments, calculated doctor time and cost involved in walking and looking for patients, measured patient satisfaction with a simple survey, and figured increased lab costs. Finally, we looked at patient dangers when a necessary test was repeatedly postponed. All of this information was already available and, anecdotally, everyone agreed that the present method was ineffective and dangerous. Still, it didn't get approval for change.

So we didn't change. We did a small *test* of change. We started with the smallest possible sample. We tried a new approach with one patient. That patient was given a fixed time and place that was guaranteed. The doctor knew in advance where they would be and when. We prepared two kits for each patient. One was the clinical kit including everything needed for the procedure. The other was the paperwork kit, including the template for the letter to the family physician and the surveys for the patient and the doctor.

The initial test was done with the doctor who had the idea. We were able to find a bed we could use for the entire test period of 18 days. The first two days, we saw only one patient per day, went through the process and made any changes we could see to the kits and procedure. Then we tried two patients per day. We made changes that scaling up suggested. Then we included other doctors and made improvements they suggested. After a week, we added the third daily patient and continued making improvements to the end of our small test.

We took the records we had of the successful test to the manager. We made the presentation just for her. She was the first person in the bureaucracy who needed to sign off on the permanent change. So we paid attention to how she liked to get her data. She preferred visual charts to spreadsheets so we made a lot of colorful comparisons. Patient satisfaction scores had gone through the roof, but her real focus was on cost savings so we made sure those numbers were front and center.

What we did was dramatically different from previous efforts with the bureaucracy. We were presenting data from an actual test and not a new idea we wanted to try. We hadn't changed anything yet. We had simply done a small test of change and measured it against the current way of doing things.

All the questions and objections were already handled in the test. "What if..." questions that halt most new initiatives were already tested and answered. ("What if the patients don't like this new system?" "What if the lab objects?")

She still wasn't happy making changes on her own, though. She told us to go to the COO. We made an additional presentation just for the COO that included her preferences. We also included in her presentation the triggers we knew the CEO and medical director would focus on. We assumed our presentation would be passed around so we designed it to talk to all the people we guessed might be asked to take a look. It only took a few days and we got approval to make our small test permanent. They even found a small amount of money to help convert a room in the ward. Now we had a permanent bed in the neurological unit that allowed two or even three lumbar punctures to be done smoothly every day. No running around, no waiting, no delays, lower cost, and happier and healthier patients.

CHAPTER 23

Plan, Do, Study, Act

The task seemed clear and simple. Devise a form the hospital could use to assess patient wellness. The idea was to get better at quickly determining who was improving and who was failing. The man taking on the task had vast experience in healthcare, excellent communication skills, and a mind perfectly tuned to understand and improve processes. He watched and interviewed nurses, doctors, and patients. He took detailed notes. After mocking up the new form, he tested it by shadowing some nurses and doctors for a few days.

Satisfied that he had nailed it, he printed up a thousand forms, took them to three wards, and asked that they be used, in place of the old form, from that point on. It didn't work. The form was rejected within a week. Professionals were upset, patients were put in danger, and his competence was called into question.

The reasons for the failure were subtle. The form was designed to be filled out by someone who thought like he did. Most people weren't that organized. It didn't take into account how a busy nurse would see the questions or check boxes.

Anyone implementing change must treat failure as information to be used. They must see breakdowns as chances to improve the system.

Doctors found the form too restrictive. They didn't have enough room to write what they wanted to share. A few key points were left off the form or were difficult to locate and so they were missed. And other wards, based on their specific patient needs, had even more problems. The surgical and children's ward found the form useless because it didn't come close to covering the situations they saw regularly.

But all that didn't matter. *Nobody* could have done it the way he tried to do it. So many variables in such a complex system meant it had to be done using small tests of change.

Any change in a complex system will create unforeseen circumstances. It will also create unexpected failures. In hospitals, failure can cause injury or death, so it's vitally important any change be tested before broad implementation.

Good planners pride themselves on being able to predict what might go wrong and avoid it. But this doesn't work on two levels. First, no one can predict how a change in a complex system will alter the outcome. Second, people who believe they are smart enough to avoid failures tend not to see them when they appear. This dangerous blindness means they continue to implement mistakes and people continue to be harmed by them.

Anyone implementing change must treat failure as information to be used. They must see breakdowns as chances to improve the system.

This is especially important when working with multiple professions in one process. When a change crosses multiple professions, barriers and the odds of failure rise dramatically.

In a hospital, most processes cross multiple professions. Even a small improvement will have to work for surgeons, nurses, transport aides, administrators, and anesthetists. You can't use theory to convince such a diverse group about the benefit of a change. You need to show the actual change.

The PDSA approach is one way. It stands for Plan, Do, Study, Act.

Looking at our example, the first part of *planning* would be to discover precisely what the problems were with the existing system. Who was suffering, what were the costs, what were the arguments for change? That information would make the case for change among those who would have to get used to the new form and the bureaucracy that would have to approve the new approach. It would also provide the needed points for the test version of the form.

The *doing* part of this process requires very careful testing under controlled conditions. In a hospital something this critical should be limited to one patient on one day under close supervision. The form would be used, perhaps in parallel to the old approach, while doing detailed observation. Notes and video would prepare for the next step.

We need to *study* the outcomes. What worked? What was too hard to use? Was anything missed? What would the people using the form change? After everyone had their say, the form is adjusted and plans made for the next test.

Then, *acting* on the new data, another test is performed under the same controlled conditions. And the cycle is repeated.

Once the form reaches a point where no more changes are requested, it's tested with two patients on the ward — under the same cautious conditions.

After we've gone a week with two patients and no changes, it's time to double the count and go to four patients.

All this time data is gathered to show the benefit of the chosen approach. When everyone is comfortable with the safety and usefulness of the form in the hands of all potential users, then it's time to print it and distribute it on that ward only.

Although it's tempting to make something like this uniform, not everything is improved by uniformity. One nurse asked, "Do you expect me to put a child's life in danger so it's easier for somebody, somewhere to build a database?" Clearly geriatric, neurology, surgical, and children's wards will all have different signs that a patient is doing well or is failing. The steps have to be followed in each ward that has a different protocol for patients. The wellness indicators for a pediatric ward are vastly different from a neurological ward where many are in a coma.

This approach gives you the best chance of both producing something useful and having it used, since in each place the people using it have a hand in its creation.

CHAPTER 24

How Fast Can a Team Go?

I heard a story about a leadership school run in the American Southwest. I've not been able to verify it, but I like the way the story sounds.

The school takes place on a two-week backcountry trip. Everyone is given the same instruction in advance about the right clothing to wear, the importance of wearing broken-in footwear, the need to be in good shape. The night before the start of the program, the assembled group goes over all the important facts again and anyone who wants to drop out is given a chance to do so with a full refund. If someone thinks they over-estimated their skills or readiness, there is no shame in getting out now.

The next morning, the leader takes them out to the departure point in the desert, points them toward a butte in the distance, and tells them their job is to hike the trail to that butte before sundown, set up their tent, cook their dinner, and wait for him. Then he drives off.

It's obvious right away who is in great shape with good equipment. They take the lead and disappear fairly quickly. The second group has no real problems, they

A team can only go as fast as its slowest necessary member.

just move more slowly. But there is always a third group that isn't doing so well. Some are more strongly affected by the heat, some get blisters, some just don't have the energy. The third group is in serious danger of not making it to the goal.

In each of these groups are people who are simply trying to make the goal in a very challenging situation. And there are also people who look around them to see how others are doing and see if they can help. These are the people who offer a spare hat, a cool drink, or help treat and prevent blisters. This group stays with the slow and injured people and makes sure they make it to camp. Sometimes they make a drag and carry someone into camp. Others can make it to the destination on their own, but need help setting up their tent and feeding themselves.

No one is in danger. The leader and his staff are watching from a distance and at any point can drive a seriously endangered student back to the base and medical care.

In the evening, the instructor arrives and brings the entire group together around a campfire. He invites the people who arrived early with strength to spare to sit at his right and everyone else to sit where they wanted.

Then he does something that surprises everyone. He calls out the names of the people who were last or who needed help and asks them to name the people who helped them. Each helper stands as they are named. The instructor announces that those standing will be his leaders for the next two weeks.

He turns to those sitting at his right and asks them what they were thinking. "You are on a leadership course. Who did you think you were leading? What did you think the job of the leader was? To show how great you are? To prove you are stronger than everyone else? Did you really think your job was to abandon the weak and unprepared?"

Too often that is the chosen role of the leader. They see their job as proving their strength and skill rather than helping every member of the team make their contribution. But here is the most important fact to know about a team:

A team can only go as fast as its slowest necessary member.

Roll that over in your mind for a minute. Once you have your team free of extraneous members, the rest can only go as fast as the slowest. You can leave that slow person behind, drag them by the hair or throw them ahead, but all those actions cause damage and mean that a necessary member of the team will not make their contribution. That means your team will fail.

Whether you are team leader or a member, it's your job to take care of the slowest necessary team members among you and make sure they are able to make their contribution. Anything less guarantees failure.

CHAPTER 25

Relationships Make It All Work

Maintenance in a factory is essential if we are to keep the machines running. If you are in charge of those machines and don't do the maintenance, you'll be fired. We need to think about human maintenance just as clearly. Human beings need care. We must treat them with respect and a clear knowledge of when they need help or rest. To do that, we have to be as close to the people as a mechanic is to the machine.

We need to know when there is a bad vibration or overheating. We can't do that without the intimate act of listening that leads to understanding, which leads to relationship.

It's common wisdom, especially if you are elevated to management, that you can't be friends with your co-workers. This is completely wrong, very damaging, and totally unnecessary.

It's based on the assumption that if you are friends you won't be able to do the difficult things a manager or co-worker might have to do. Some also worry that a closer relationship might allow a worker to take advantage of them. They worry that a good relationship

When you look at the foundations of work in almost any organization, you find relationships.

might prevent them from having necessary and difficult conversations.

First, friends don't have a problem when a friend speaks honestly to them. When it's clear you are doing your management job and doing it as a friend, you are actually more effective than if you have withdrawn into some cold place where you announce managerial edicts.

Second, friends don't take advantage of friends in that way. If someone tries to abuse their relationship with you as a co-worker, they are not a friend.

We love to look at systems and processes as the reason things get done in an organization. It gives us a sense of predictability and order.

But when you look at the foundations of work in almost any organization, you find relationships. People who know and respect each other will go out of their way to do the work. People who don't know or don't care will do the minimum. When something goes wrong, if we know the people involved, we will come to their aid. If they are unknown, or worse, from a competing department, we might just do nothing and wait for them to sink.

Production suffers when relationships suffer. But there's something even worse than that. We spend most of our waking hours at work. We are with our co-workers more than we are with our children or our partner. We see our significant other and children for a few tired hours at the end of the day.

If we are going to remain distant from the people with whom we spend most of our waking hours, who are we in relationship with?

The people we work with determine if we have a sense of accomplishment at the end of the day or the year. They often determine the quality of our other relationships. It's common for frustrated and angry people to take out those feelings on those closest to them. Families and friends suffer when work is a torment.

On the other side, when we are happy and fulfilled in our work we are much more pleasant to be around. So it makes great sense to invest in those relationships.

I'm not saying you have to have your co-workers over to your place on a regular basis. It's also true, since you can't choose your co-workers, sometimes you'll be working closely with someone you truly don't want to have a close relationship with. But that's no excuse for not trying. You're going to be next to them anyway. Warming up the relationship will benefit everyone.

When did it become lame to say you love your work or your co-workers? I think the word and the idea of love has been artificially driven from the workplace. It's labeled as being unprofessional or weird. But if we accept that love is one of the most powerful forces in the human experience, how can we remove it from difficult activities where we spend most of our time? Why would we do that? Reverse it. Take an interest in your co-workers. Make the work personal and enjoy the relationships.

I believe the biggest illness of our time is loneliness. There are more of us packed closer together with more technology to connect us than ever before. And we are more lonely than we have ever been. So step out and connect. It won't always go smoothly — friendships and relationships all have their problems. But the benefit of more connections and more meaning in your life are worth the risk and the cost.

CHAPTER 26

How Many Spaces Are Between Your Toes?

When I was promoted from Assistant Director to Director of Development at the public television station, I had to do something I'd never done before. I had to hire someone — my replacement. I did what I could to get ready. I read a number of books and articles on hiring. I studied advertisements and spoke to my colleagues. Finally, I placed the ad and waited for the résumés.

From my reading, I'd created a list of questions that I wanted to ask each applicant. I'd like to think I was listening, but the truth is I didn't know what I was listening for. I went through the motions and made notes on each person's résumé after they left. Nobody was standing out.

Then a man arrived who I thought was a little older than me. He seemed good-humored and comfortable in the interview. That stood in contrast to all the nervousness I'd already witnessed.

I was enjoying the conversation and was about halfway through my questions when he stopped me. "These

"I can't work with you. You're too boring." He walked out.

questions are boring. I thought you wanted a creative person." I told him that was exactly what I wanted. "No, you don't. If you wanted someone creative, you'd ask questions that reflected that."

I was really intrigued. What kind of questions?

"I don't know. Questions that showed how people think, for example. You might ask me how many spaces I have between my toes. You would then know how I solved such a problem. Do I look up to the left and close my eyes? Do I look at my hand as an analog? Do I take off my shoes and socks and count? Just one shoe or both? This would get you some real information." I was getting really excited about this approach so I asked for more and he gave me a similar question.

"You could ask how many sides, edges and corners there are in a cube. One way to answer is to pick something cube-like off the desk. Another way would be to recognize that we are talking inside a cube. All I'm saying is you could be more creative in your questions."

I tried to craft a few more creative questions on the spot, but I didn't really succeed. Still, I was so impressed with what I heard that I offered him the job on the spot.

He turned me down. "I can't work with you. You're too boring." He walked out. I felt like I had just been given my first master class in how to hire a great person. I've used the lessons I learned from that one interview in every hiring situation since.

One of the more destructive parts of hiring is that the first step is usually to screen people out of the process rather than screening people into the job. We start off looking for what disqualifies a candidate. If their résumé doesn't include some key words, activities or titles, they go on the rejected pile. For example, I might look for a degree in something possibly related to the job listing when really that degree has nothing to do with someone's ability to do the work.

I understand why it's done. It makes deciding who to meet in person easier by making the résumé pile very small very quickly. But it doesn't really accomplish the task.

If I were looking to screen people in, I'd be looking at the characteristics a person would need and try to find a positive match. If the job requires the person be innovative and work in a team, I would look for that first rather than after I'd thinned the list by rejecting people for lack of credentials.

This is true for a lot of interviews. Either the questions are boring or they're designed to confuse or challenge the candidate. Some firms seem to do really well in matching their job listing, their screening, and their interviews to get the right person in the right job. Other firms spend almost no time thinking on their own about what qualities they are looking for and how they'll illuminate them. They think if they use Google's or Microsoft's interview questions they are ahead of the game.

That approach requires you to buy into two assumptions: The first is that the questions work for the company you borrowed them from, and the second is that you're looking for the same characteristics they're looking for. Having both those assumptions be true is highly unlikely.

We really need to consider what would make a person successful in the job or jobs they would be asked to do. Is there a team? How does it function? How is leadership expressed and acknowledged in our company? What strengths do those who are now succeeding demonstrate? What weaknesses have caused otherwise excellent candidates to be short-timers? What attributes, both skills and temperament, are we going to need over the next few years?

When we have a handle on those, we can begin to craft questions and conversations that truly give us a window into the characteristics and potential success of the person in front of us.

This approach does take more time initially. It's especially time consuming when you do it right and have a candidate interviewed by the people they'll be working with, not just the boss or hiring manager. But in the end, it takes a fraction of the time and cost of hiring, training, trying, and losing a candidate.

CHAPTER 27

Lead With What You Have

I had the opportunity to work with a large communications organization that had offices all over the world. My focus was the Orlando and New Jersey offices, and my job was to try and help them do their work more effectively. The work product (internal software) from the New Jersey offices was awful. It was full of mistakes and often caused serious problems for the company.

By contrast, the work product coming out of the Florida office was outstanding. It was always on time and of high quality. I focused on what was different and was surprised to see how much difference the furniture made.

These subsidiaries were required to use the same cubicle furniture and they were in roughly the same kinds of buildings — plain office park buildings. But the similarities ended there.

The first thing you saw when you entered the New Jersey building was the list of notices describing all the things you couldn't do or that were illegal. Parking rules, a harassment notice, an overtime notice, refrigerator regulations. That was your welcome. There was no visible receptionist. You had to find your way to a senior office and there, in her own cubicle, was the executive assistant who could tell you who was in or out if she phoned them.

The cubicle furniture was laid out in rows with staggered doors so you could walk past the fewest number of cubicles and risk seeing few people. You could get to your desk, work all day, and leave without ever interacting with anyone. If you wanted to see others, you could go to the coffee room, which was a converted janitor closet and held one person comfortably. You were meant to get your coffee and go. There was no group place to sit.

Senior members of staff had the offices around the perimeter, and those doors were mostly kept closed. When I asked why, they said because of noise, although there wasn't much noise. It reminded me of a tomb. No loud voices and certainly no laughter.

Now to Florida. Remember, these were employees of the same company in the same kind of building and using the same cubicle furniture.

When you entered the Florida offices, the first thing you saw was a large photo wall of everyone who worked there, their first and last names and what they did. To the left of this was a desk sitting out in the open with the receptionist. Just like in the north, she did double duty acting as the executive assistant for 95% of the day and greeting the odd person who came in off the street.

Using the cubicle furniture in a different way, they made two large courtyards with cubicles around them and anchored the whole area with a couch and a coffee pot in the center. To get to your desk, you had to enter the courtyard. Everyone saw you come in or leave. Conversations took place across the courtyard. There were no rules about what you could talk about, but they focused mostly on work. There is a reason for this. These people were proud of the work they did. Since they had that personal pride, they had no interest in wasting time. Of course, they would catch up with each other and pay attention and laugh and goof off from time to time, but their focus was on doing excellent work.

I heard many spirited conversations and arguments about projects and approaches. I heard a lot of laughter and I heard a lot of discussions that solved problems in an instant which, in a more isolating environment like the one in New Jersey, would almost certainly be handled with a series of emails. They simply talked with each other.

One of the big problems of an open office is noise and distraction. They had two solutions for this. The first was the unwritten rule that if your back was to the

Using the cubicle furniture in a different way, they made two large courtyards with cubicles around them and anchored the whole area with a couch and a coffee pot in the center.

cubicle opening, you were busy and not to be disturbed.

The second was to take any large or loud meetings to a conference room.

The offices at the perimeter were not assigned to senior managers. One was a lunch room. Most of the rest were conference rooms for larger and rowdier group needs. A couple were small offices for when someone visited and needed a private place to work or when a manager had to talk privately to someone.

The boss took an office near the front, but I didn't see him there very often. Usually he was out and about, either on the floor with the people doing the work or visiting with the customers of his work. He gained constant and useful information by listening and watching.

Of the two places, it was pretty obvious Orlando was where people wanted to work. They enjoyed coming in to work, enjoyed each other's company, and were proud of what they did. What else could you ask for in a job?

Well, the boss gave them more.

The boss carried small rewards with him at all times. He might have cinema passes, restaurant vouchers, or other gift certificates. They weren't bank-breaking, but they cost enough to be meaningful. I asked him what budget line these rewards came out of, since I knew this company was not the type to support his approach. He told me he paid for them himself. When I suggested that was a lot of money to come out of his own pocket, he just laughed. It was a deep belly laugh.

"Do you know how many raises and promotions these people have given me? Do you know how many nights and weekends I'm *not* disturbed because this group is happy to handle problems?" He figured the rewards hadn't cost him a penny.

Then he told me how he handed them out. It wasn't anything like the Employee of the Month fiasco that many companies try. Since he was walking around all the time, he witnessed people doing the right things all the time. When he did see something he appreciated, he would pull out one of these rewards and give it to the person right then with a heartfelt "thank you." It was very powerful. And the thank you, given with an appreciation for the actual work done, meant as much as the certificates.

The furniture was organized in Florida to match the philosophy of the boss. His philosophy, combined with the open and welcoming furniture arrangement, created a perfect environment that produced satisfied employees and excellent work.

If the New Jersey boss inherited the Florida layout, I predict a complete disaster, with rules going up in place of photos and common offices and conference rooms handed out to senior, not necessarily productive, employees.

If the Florida boss inherited the New Jersey layout, he would be unable to see his team working and would not interact with them in a productive way. Productivity would drop and the Florida boss would lose his joy in the work. But I'm guessing before a month was out, he would have a crew in to rearrange the furniture to suit his cooperative philosophy.

CHAPTER 28

Most Meetings Do Absolutely Nothing

What causes bad meetings? A lack of a clear purpose or agenda. The meeting room is furnished for a collection of adversaries, populated by people whose highest aspiration is making sure nothing is done that they can be blamed for. The event is led by people who do not want to be responsible for taking wrong actions.

If we're working together, we need to meet to coordinate. But when you look at the meetings you went to last week, how many would you rank as essential and how many were a waste of time? Fix or cancel meetings that are a waste of time and you'll free up a huge block of time.

Most meetings end in frustration with nothing accomplished, fingers silently pointed in blame. Secret meetings are held after the meeting to declare who was the biggest fool and share the sad feeling that we've been here and done this before and will do it again.

Is there any way out? I believe there is. Here is a simple list of rules. They aren't easy to implement in a culture that expects something else, but they are simple.

Is every attendee really essential or are they there out of habit?

Only have a meeting when there is a need. Avoid the "regular Tuesday meeting" philosophy. If you can't say why you're having the meeting, don't have it.

When you have determined the need, decide on the outcome. If you need a decision, you make that your clear outcome and you'll know if you've succeeded. If you need to share information, then make sure the attendees have understood what was shared.

Invite all the key players. Decide who is essential and let each essential person know why they are invited and what they are expected to do or bring. Cancel the meeting if an essential player isn't there. What's the point of having your meeting if you can't complete your task?

Decide the minimum attendees you can have and still reach your goal. Be creative. Is every attendee really essential or are they there out of habit? Do they attend because they represent some department that always shows up? Do you really need them at this meeting?

Once you start your meeting, proceed as if the people in the room can solve the problem. Make it clear there is no option to assign tasks to someone not in the room.

Make your meetings short. The same amount of work gets done in one-hour meetings as gets done in four-hour meetings. It all happens in the last 60 minutes, so just meet for that time. Always end meetings when you say you will.

Let everyone know that meetings will be action-oriented and that the people in the room will move forward even if others don't attend. If you only do one thing, agree on the meeting's purpose and accomplish that.

Furniture is critical. Make sure the room is set up for intimate collaboration. Large, long tables, as in a boardroom, discourage cooperation. Aim for seating people without tables. If that's not possible, arrange attendees so they don't choose sides and face off.

A facilitator doesn't need to be the senior person. Someone on staff can be charged with keeping the meeting on track and trained to ask the right questions.

If you can't have the meeting you planned to have because a key person doesn't show up, consider using part of the time to accomplish something that the assembled group *can* do. Take the time to create a new agenda for your new meeting.

I've been in a lot of companies and organizations where lousy, time-wasting meetings are considered inevitable. They don't have to be. It isn't easy to change habits, but when people see how much time you are saving them, they'll get behind any useful meeting improvement techniques.

CHAPTER 29

A Meeting Style That Works

The hospital ward where I was working cared for some of the most acute patients. They were either transferred from the emergency department or came directly from doctors or other hospitals. They arrived at all times of the day.

A hospital operates 24 hours a day, but there is still a difference between day and night shifts. Some services, like laboratory and imaging (x-ray, CT scan, MRI) have only a skeleton crew overnight. So only the highest-need patients who were admitted overnight would be scanned at 2 a.m. The rest would have a note entered in their electronic record to have an MRI, for example, when the day shift starts.

At 8 a.m. the receptionist's phone started ringing. The callers were the orderlies who were scheduled to begin moving the overnight patients to the imaging suite. They wanted to know if their first patients were wheelchair patients requiring one orderly per patient, or were they bedridden, requiring two to maneuver the bed. They also needed to know if the patient required oxygen during transport so they could bring a tank.

The orderly and the receptionist saw the answer at the same time. The orderly decided if his department knew nothing about the patient, they would send two people with wheelchairs and oxygen.

The electronic forms the doctors filled out during the night didn't have a place for this information and even if they did, the condition of these patients often changed dramatically from hour to hour. The receptionist only came on duty at 8 so she didn't know and had to track down the nurses or doctors to find out.

Three groups of people were most frustrated by this problem:

- The receptionist, who was hit by a blizzard of requests the moment she arrived.

- The orderlies, who would often bring just a wheelchair on outdated information and then have to walk back to their office, leave the wheelchair and find another orderly for bed transport. They would often have to go back to their office to pick up an oxygen tank.

- The imaging technicians, who had to wait for these delays to be resolved.

Doctors and nurses, of course, were also involved, as well as the information technology staff who maintained the reporting system. Although they were not as frustrated as the first three groups, they could have a hand in solving the problem too.

An interested and respected person from each group was invited to a meeting with special rules to see what action they could take to solve this problem. Here were the rules:

- The meeting lasts one hour. We don't go one minute past one hour. If we can't get the work done, we need another meeting.

- The meeting starts exactly on time. If the people who are there on time are convinced they can't proceed without someone who is late, the meeting is cancelled and rescheduled.

- We don't discuss solutions that require someone who isn't in the room. The actions discussed and decided are wholly in control of those in the room. If you come to the meeting, you are stating that you can decide and take action for your area.

- We can point out problems and describe them, but we waste no time in character assassination or department bashing.

We planned the meeting so the most time-starved people (doctors and nurses) could attend. But when the meeting started, we were missing representatives from the doctors, nurses, and information technology. We had someone from imaging, a senior orderly, and the receptionist. I asked if they thought they might be able to solve this without the missing professions, and they thought it might be possible. They decided to try, since they were already here.

I facilitated the meeting by outlining the problem, reminding people of the rules, and keeping the time. I used a large clock that sat in plain view.

At the beginning of the meeting, the first comments were that the electronic forms should be changed so the required data would be automatically transmitted. We stopped that discussion by reminding the group of three things. First, the IT person wasn't in the room. Second, IT was not known for fast turnaround on ideas like this. Third, the doctors would still need to fill in the data and keep it current with each patient's condition for it to mean anything. That was unlikely given the time pressures and the nature of the patients.

So the group naturally turned to the nurses to back-stop the doctors. But again, we had no nurses in the room so couldn't pursue that.

I asked the three people in the room to describe one frustrating case in detail. Then a second case. Each person had a slightly different reason for frustration, but they all seemed to hinge on the wasted time and effort of going back and forth to get the right equipment and people for transport. At about 40 minutes into the meeting, we had a clear picture of how things went wrong, but no answer on how to fix it. We had some discussion again on what potential solutions would be, coming back to earth as it was clear the people in the room couldn't implement them. At about 50 minutes, the group energy began to dissipate as they considered having another meeting.

Then I saw the solution.

My job was facilitator and not problem solver so, if I could help it, I didn't want to solve a problem they could resolve. I wanted them to have the satisfaction and confidence that working out problems brings. So I asked a question. "Is there a way we could solve this if we had no information about the patient at all? What if we didn't even have a name? How would that work?"

The orderly and the receptionist saw the answer at the same time. The orderly decided if his department knew nothing about the patient, they would send two people with wheelchairs and oxygen. If that worked for patients one and two, they would transport them both. If patient one was bedridden, they would stash the wheelchairs and use oxygen as necessary, stashing one O_2 bottle. The receptionist suggested instead they use a closet near the entrance to store a couple of wheelchairs and oxygen bottles and just send two orderlies at the start of the morning shift. They would have everything they needed to deal with whatever came up.

The three decided to test the approach under controlled conditions on a quiet day. It worked beautifully. I visited them a month later and it was still working smoothly, and even the doctors and nurses appreciated the solution, since it involved fewer interruptions.

The only person who had a problem was the receptionist. She jokingly complained that her mornings were now *too* quiet.

CHAPTER 30

Get Rid of the Furniture

Wherever there's a conflict or tension, our first instinct is to get the players around a table to talk it out. It doesn't work.

I was working with Dr. Michael Hammer on a course that employed a case study and role play. The role play was to get manufacturing and sales to come to agreement on a case problem. We assigned the roles that a small group would play — half manufacturing and half sales — and pointed them to the round table at the front of the room so they could do their negotiation in full view of the room.

They did what all normal humans do. Each tribe sat with its members on opposite sides of the table. They took their roles seriously and started talking to each other like we often see internal groups talking with each other. They made assumptions about why the "other" was doing what they did and began to throw insults at each other. At first they were gentle insults and then they escalated. We never got to see a true negotiation. We saw a normal, dysfunctional meeting.

> All the insults stopped. It turns out, even if you're angry, you're more careful with your words and more interested in a peaceful resolution when the people you are in conflict with are at each shoulder.

The next time we did the class we tried an experiment. Instead of letting the group sit where they wanted, we had a seating chart that had them alternate sales and manufacturing. We were astonished. All the insults stopped. It turns out, even if you're angry, you're more careful with your words and more interested in a peaceful resolution when the people you are in conflict with are at each shoulder.

The third time we did this the whole negotiation role play fell apart. It wasn't because they couldn't agree. Just the opposite. They agreed too quickly. Nobody got to see what actually happened. The change we had made was to remove the table and just have them sit alternately in a small circle.

I remembered this lesson when I had to facilitate a group of three CEOs. Each of them was the head of a hospital that were all being combined into one unit.

They all wanted the top job, and they didn't trust the motives of the others. This led to a lack of cooperation and a delay in important combinations of services. They would have to cooperate or there would be serious issues for patients.

I invited them to a conference area that I prepared. The seats they would occupy were placed so they sat knee-to-knee. I had a maintenance man help me move heavy concrete planters behind the chairs so they couldn't enlarge the space. You might laugh, but they tried to move them. I asked them to stop and just try the layout as it was.

I had a couple of questions for them that I hoped would let them see the sincerity of the others. I asked them to answer two questions: "What do you want?" and "How do you feel?"

They did this exercise for an hour. The topics that fit into these two simple questions are infinite. Conversation moved from personal needs to logistical worries, from career concerns to area public health. It was a satisfying hour and they certainly got to know each other and their motives better.

Did it stop the competition and jockeying for position? Of course not! These were driven and competitive men who always had to know what the right thing was. But it did improve understanding and it showed them that, for an hour at least, they could work together on common problems.

Eventually none of them got the overall job. That went to someone who came from outside the group.

Even the most aggressive and competitive people will calm down and be reasonable if they are within smacking distance of each other. When you want to get people to slow down and approach agreement, take away the furniture and let cooperative human nature take over.

CHAPTER 31

There Is No Change Management

Anyone who has experienced change in a complex system like a large organization knows the tools of management don't begin to cover the need. Change is complex, chaotic, disruptive, and unpredictable. The moment you perturb a complex system you have altered it and its output beyond any planning you could have done.

Only the tools of leadership are useful during change. You have to fix your eyes on an outcome, take chances, constantly adjust, and deal with failures, setbacks, and completely unforeseen circumstances. You cannot ask for dramatic change and then, when it comes, expect to manage it.

You must appeal to leaders in your organization to make change work. I wish there were a simple prescription of how to be successful in change leadership, but that would be like giving a simple explanation of leadership.

The best I can do is a simple explanation of a leader. A leader is a person who has willing followers. People

Only the tools of leadership are useful during change. You have to fix your eyes on an outcome, take chances, constantly adjust, and deal with failures, setbacks, and completely unforeseen circumstances.

become willing followers when they see the benefits of the destination you describe and trust that you are the person who can lead them there.

When you begin to explore a change you'll find people break into roughly three categories.

The first is the group who loves the idea and will support it wholeheartedly. Some of them like the idea, some like you, but their support is a lock. The second and largest group is unsure. They can be persuaded but they aren't yet. Listening to their concerns and improvements will get them on board for at least the start of the initiative.

And then there are the people who are not going to support the initiative. Some will join after its worth has been proven and some will never be in support. Some of this group will have to leave, either to another company or another area.

One of the primary tasks of the leader bringing in a new initiative is convincing the second group to work for its success. Here are the main steps.

Identify the leaders of this group. These are not the people necessarily on the top of the org chart, but are the ones others go to with questions or problems.

Ask them to tell you under what circumstances this initiative would be beneficial to them. Ask if they can see a way to achieve those circumstances. You are essentially asking them, "What do you think?"

Ask them to talk about their experience in change initiatives. What went wrong? What made it go wrong? What would they do to keep the present initiative on track?

Share with them what is likely to happen with this initiative. You are certain, for example, that the energy at the start will fall off. You know that any changes to a complex system will make your plans out of date as soon as you begin. You know the timeline you worked so hard on will need adjustment. These things are not failures, but are predictable results of change.

Ask if you can call on them as these predictable "failures" cause others to lose their momentum.

Ask these leaders to identify the most thoughtful skeptics in their group. There is a good chance they themselves are the skeptics, but you want to know all of them. You need the skeptics since they sway a very large group.

Have the same conversation with the skeptics.

Then don't talk any more about the initiative until you have taken some actions that make it real. Once people in the organization begin to talk about what you're doing (even if the talk is mostly complaints), you can announce your initiative.

So what can you expect from change? You can expect the unexpected. You cannot plan the steps of change. Well, that's not completely true. You can plan the first step. And you might be able to predict the reaction to that first step. After that the crystal ball becomes murky.

Here are a few things that might show up.

People who were on board at the beginning will get cold feet, wonder why this thing has gone so wrong and insist that, although they supported something, it was never this.

ACTION: Let people know in advance they are signing up for something that will certainly go off in unexpected directions. Part of the job of anyone who signs up now is to recognize when that has happened and figure out the best next step.

People will ask you for your timeline. When an uncontrollable complex system changes your timeline, they want to find the failure.

ACTION: Before starting any initiative, get the advice of anyone who will be in this fault-finding position later. Ask them to tell you their experience with projects like this. You will hear them tell you about these same kinds of "failures." Write down what you hear and send it later as an email. In that email ask if you might call on them for help when you get to the inevitable sticky situations.

Concentrating your energy on the skeptics and uncertain supporters gives you a group who will be more interested in success than complaining. They give you a shot at leading change.

Leadership is a complicated dance and not everyone wants to dance. It's easy to be swept up by the enthusiasm of the small group of people who are instantly on board. But in change you will have to lead the majority of people — the large middle group who is not convinced. You cannot manage them. They must want to follow your lead.

CHAPTER 32

There Are No Mergers

I was speaking with a group about cooperating with another department when they told me they just couldn't. "They don't think like us. They are really from a different company." They *were* from a different company: one that had been a part of a "merger" 25 years before.

We often hear about mergers and the wonderful things the companies are going to do together. We hear the word "synergy" a lot. By combining intelligence and departments, eliminating duplication, and joining hands, the merged group will move gracefully toward a profitable future.

It doesn't work. Some "merged" groups still have the pre-merger boundaries many years after the combination.

Almost every merger is, in reality, a takeover. In take-overs, there is a winner and a loser. And no matter what you call it, everyone knows if they are in the winner or loser category. If you are in the winner camp, you can't help but act like it. And if you are one of the losers, you'll act defiant or oppressed or both.

They have, and will always have, a different past. The goal of new leadership is to help them create a common future that honors their respective pasts.

Victors swagger. This is even worse if the victors don't assume their role honestly. If they quietly swagger through the halls and only pull rank occasionally, they cannot be trusted. "We are all in this together" becomes "Do it my way!" whenever there is conflict. This quickly demonstrates that we are not all in this together. You are working for us.

Most communication in this situation is weak or lies. People will talk about synergy and a new age and then do nothing to bring the groups together. They have, and will always have, a different past. The goal of new leadership is to help them create a common future that honors their respective pasts.

History is not a small thing. We often define ourselves by what we've done, and organizations, being made up of people, do the same thing. So to be told that your past is now gone and you are a part of a new organization is just not easy to take. It's like being told of a death with no funeral to go to. It's worse than that. On top of no funeral, you're expected to celebrate the arrival and ascendance of strangers at the moment you feel like grieving.

There is a way to reduce these problems. Acknowledge the death of the old company by having a "funeral." Publicly acknowledge the death of the old organization. Create visual celebrations of past successes (like display cases and web sites) that remain visible for years.

There is no guarantee this will allow everyone to move on and join the new organization. Not everyone moves on even years after the death of a loved one. But this approach at least honors past contributions and has the chance of reducing resentment in a group of people who have earned pride in past accomplishments.

If it's a takeover, be honest about it. Creating placating language does nothing to soothe the true wounds. Often nobody is clear who is authorized to make the tough decisions. The winner group has clear leaders. The loser group still has leaders, but their authority is now murky. Many decisions go unmade because everyone is waiting for clarity or new direction.

Make it clear how decisions will be made. If the victors are making all the rules, don't offend people's intelligence by pretending otherwise.

Culture is not a small thing. All of the little things that make an organization work become problems when they are questioned or removed after the takeover. How a group hires, how they conduct meetings, how they celebrate retirements, are part of how people see themselves. Forced culture changes create resentment and hostility.

There will be conflict and disagreement among departments for as long as there are organizations. But pretending there has been a wonderful union while ignoring the loss a large part of the group feels just leads to disaster and very long-term conflict and grief.

CHAPTER 33

Accidental Communication Plan

I worked with a top leader at an insurance company who wanted to shift the approach of his organization from a hierarchical to a more team-led orientation. This wasn't easy since they had a long history of top-down focus to overcome. But the leader was insistent and got the message out that everyone should try.

Most managers declined to commit themselves to the change. They held back, offered heartfelt lip service, and waited for the whole thing to blow over. There was no danger in this. They didn't fight the change. They just didn't put any energy into it. They kept producing in the traditional way so there would be no question about their value.

But Barbara decided the boss had a good idea and really pushed herself. She spent time with her team to teach them what the new world expected of them. She herself did the hard work of letting some of the work move to her team and did not pull it back when she got nervous they might be doing it wrong. She decided that as long as everyone knew what the goals were, she would

Action is the only communication plan.

be happy to get there, even if at first it looked unfamiliar and was a little bit slower.

There were some setbacks, but overall her team was successful and they were getting faster. You could say they were making their mistakes faster and then fixing them faster.

All of this was expected with a change of this magnitude. But the boss wasn't paying attention to his own feelings about the change. He prided himself on doing things well. If he wasn't a perfectionist, then he was close to it. It's understandable. He worked in an area where even small mistakes could cost millions. The mistakes this team were making weren't the kind that threatened the business. Barbara didn't allow them to make fatal mistakes. They were simply learning their way to a new way of working, and they didn't always get it right the first time.

I was asked to visit the boss on Monday morning and talk with him about his communication plan for getting more people moving on the team approach. When I got to the office, I heard Barbara had been demoted.

When I met the boss he was eager to get started on the communication plan, but I assured him it was already complete and in action. He wanted to know what the hell I was talking about. "You demoted Barbara. That says everything anyone here needs to know about the wisdom of following the team approach."

He wanted to argue. He told me it was a lateral move and we jousted about that for awhile. I asked him if he'd had Barbara's job and was moved into the one she has now would he feel promoted or demoted. His silence was his agreement.

"So everyone who was watching to see how you treated your most enthusiastic supporter of teamwork now knows. Nobody will do this now unless you make a drastic U-turn with Barbara and admit you made a mistake. You probably have to appoint her to a more senior position than she had before, just to make the point."

He was a proud man and he couldn't see himself doing that. And that was the end of the communication plan.

I know there is some value in formal communication plans as templates for action. I've seen them work in that capacity. But people don't really care what you write, or how many videos you make. They only really care what you do. Action is the only communication plan.

CHAPTER 34

Let the Employees Do the Employee Survey

Organizations are always talking about their openness to change, but they seldom mean it. Most groups are so wrapped up in keeping safe they have forgotten their courage. You can see it in how they treat new hires and even in the kinds of people they hire and promote. The people fit a comfortable template, and when they arrive they don't rock the boat. If they are likely to rock the boat, they are quickly put in their place or removed.

Companies that are serious about positive change listen to their employees even when what they hear is uncomfortable.

I was working with a large financial services firm that was having problems on a number of levels. They were losing clients, losing money, and losing key staff.

I asked if there was an employee survey. "Yes, we do one every year," was the reply. Could I review it? No, only a few people get to see the results. I asked if I could see anonymized copies of employee exit interviews. No, those are never seen outside HR. Do we have

Companies that are serious about positive change listen to their employees even when what they hear is uncomfortable.

any data on customer dissatisfaction? An uncomfortable silence. Would they mind if I spoke with some present and previous customers? Well, we don't really do that. So without data, what is it you want to change? I asked again if I could get a look at a recent employee survey and was told I could look at a summary.

The summary they showed me had been produced so there would be no discomfort for anyone reading it. They simply removed anything that wasn't positive and put a positive spin on anything they couldn't ignore. Some questions were removed altogether.

So I got to see things like: "Sixty-three percent of respondents agreed with the statement that 'Our company is a great place to work.'" When I looked at the survey the employees were sent, I found they were asked to place that statement on a five-point scale from strongly agree to strongly disagree. Digging deeper, I found that anything from the middle or higher was considered a positive statement. Forty-two percent of those positives fell into the middle category.

This is a great place to work:

STRONGLY AGREE	5%
AGREE	16%
NOT SURE	42%
DISAGREE	8%
STRONGLY DISAGREE	29%

63% THINK IT'S A GREAT PLACE TO WORK

79% THINK IT ISN'T

This was a disaster hidden in cooked numbers. By taking the "not sure" number and adding it to the disagree numbers instead, you could just as easily say that 79 percent *didn't* think it was a great place to work.

In any case, access to the information was so restricted that few people knew what it said and nobody was really interested in doing anything with the data anyway.

If you really want to see what employees think, keep your employee survey out of the hands of HR. The job of HR is a tough balance between helping the employees be successful and protecting the company.

Change the game. Let the staff create the survey. There is a science to crafting a good survey, of course. Leading questions can skew results and make a bad survey dangerous. Let them use tools like Survey Monkey that include templates and questions that allow anyone to put together a good survey. These services are extremely affordable.

Have the employees complete the survey and compile the results. Then do something about the obvious problems. For more complex or nuanced problems, talk with them about what actions could be taken to improve things.

Be aware you're going to have to follow through. If employees say you should implement a nurse's evaluation of doctors, then do it. If the doctors want to evaluate admin, then do it.

Don't ask employees if you don't want to know. But if you do ask them, you have to do something about the problems they bring to you.

CHAPTER 35

Organizations Are Not Machines

A short time ago I had a problem with the juniper bushes lining our driveway. The thick, woody parts were a hazard that had already damaged a bumper and cost us a tail light. I decided to prune.

Mature junipers have a solid green top that looks like it goes on forever. But one cut and I found I had removed the only living part of the plant, leaving a lifeless support structure exposed.

It was a living organism and my simple cut damaged parts I never intended to harm. The same thing happens every day in organizations.

There is a lot of desire to boil organizations down to their activities so planners can easily understand them and fix whatever might be broken. We might focus on processes or sub-processes or even re-engineering. But a machine isn't the right analog for an organization made up of people. The right analog is a living being.

You can cut costs with a chain saw and fail, or you can reduce costs the same amount in the same timeframe and thrive.

They say it takes courage and wisdom to cut what is almost entirely employees. No, it's a lazy approach and a complete abdication of leadership.

The ones who fail look at the required savings and make a blanket announcement that every department has to cut their budget by 25%.

Whenever a company makes these kinds of cuts, the stock market seems to reward them. They say it takes courage and wisdom to trim what is almost entirely employees.

No, it's a lazy approach and a complete abdication of leadership. First, the leader has to be able to act strategically in moments of crisis. Where do they make money and where do they lose? What will be different five or ten years from now?

It might make more sense to remove entire departments than to force everyone to cut 25%.

Good leaders ask the people doing the work where they can save money. They let them do the more detailed work of finding sensible areas to cut. Bad leaders figure they and their reports know exactly how to trim the living being. They will almost certainly get that wrong.

Good leadership doesn't hinge on the ability to be ruthless. Changing the shape or the size of an organization requires skill and wisdom if the new organization is to survive. Changing the model from machine to living being gives any leader a workable template that magnifies their skill and wisdom.

CHAPTER 36

Bureaucracy Is Your Friend

I worked on an iron ore freighter on the Great Lakes one year. These ships are long and heavy. Although I worked the deck, I was invited one day to the bridge to take a turn at steering the ship. My experience there is a perfect metaphor, I think, for what it's like to change the direction of any large organization.

There were no fixed points on the sunny morning I was at the wheel. We were in the middle of Lake Michigan so I wasn't in any danger of crashing into anything. The mate asked me to use the compass to turn the ship 10 degrees to starboard. I turned the wheel and waited almost 30 seconds before any movement occurred. I should have turned the wheel back as soon as the compass started to move, but I was new at this. The mate just smiled as the ship went way past 10 degrees. Now he asked me to get back on the original heading. I made the same mistake, overcorrecting, trying to make this huge ship turn the way I wanted it to go, right away. I spent about 45 minutes narrowing down my course corrections before he took over again.

Think of bureaucracy as the huge section of a ship that's underwater. Without it, the ship would be top

> **The same structure that gives us stability makes it difficult to change course.**
>
>

heavy and unstable and would roll over and sink in minutes. Also, if the ship didn't have that large part underwater, it would be blown across the sea with ease. Without bureaucracy, there would be no stability.

So, when we see a bureaucracy and get angry, we're just missing the point. Bureaucracy is us trying to keep a sense of order as we attempt to guide something huge through necessary change. Without it, we'd be sunk. On the other hand, the same structure that gives us stability makes it difficult to change course.

Organizations move the same way. You can pull all the levers, turn all the wheels that should change the direction and nothing seems to happen. Then, suddenly, things start to move. Then you try to control them and all hell breaks loose. It goes too far and you over-correct. It's not coming back to center so you pull harder and even smash the wheel in frustration.

There is an easier way.

First, you have to recognize the attributes of a bureaucracy and work with them. Here they are.

1. IT DOESN'T LIKE SURPRISES. A bureaucracy is the ultimate management tool. It's not intended as a leadership tool. It depends on doing things in a certain way. Any variation from the normal method is seen as a threat and is wrong.

2. IT DOESN'T LIKE CHANGE. The first and only answer to the question, "Can we change this?" is "No!" It has to be that way, if you think about it. It may not be working well, but whatever it is, it is working. And even if it's broken, we're not going to risk making it more broken.

3. IT DOESN'T LIKE RISK. The whole point of a bureaucracy is reducing or eliminating risk, so of course it doesn't like risk.

So whatever you introduce to the bureaucracy has to come as no surprise, seem like a normal progression rather than change, and present no risk.

If it's your job in the bureaucracy to maintain stability and you're not sure a new approach will enhance stability, you can kill most new ideas by asking a few "what if" questions. By the time you get to the third question with no answers, everyone agrees that it's better to just "put this aside for now since we don't seem to have the information we need to make a good decision."

As someone who wants to make the bureaucracy a partner, you just have to follow these rules.

1. Never talk about your idea with an "approver" until you have done your small test of change. If you need approval to do the test then make sure to make your request as easy to approve as possible. Make it clear it's only a test, it will be done with complete focus on safety and security, and nothing will change until the data from the test is analyzed and a course of action approved.

2. Do your test with the greatest care. You want your first test to be small and outside the stream of daily activity if possible. In other words, what you are doing in the test runs parallel to daily production — it doesn't replace it.

3. Make your presentation match the listening preferences of the person or group that must say yes. Make the results of your test clear at a glance. Use graphs, pictures, stories, and spreadsheets so you cover the bases.

4. If you think your proposal might be passed around, make it work for those you predict will see it.

5. Be prepared for the approver to say no. If they do, ask them specifically what their concern is. Listen carefully, take notes, and then do another test. Answer any concerns that come up with another test. Don't be defensive in the meeting.

Bureaucracies can truly work in your favor if you work with them to get a result that improves the organization.

When you dance with the bureaucracy instead of banging on the door demanding that it change, you can accomplish any improvement.

CHAPTER 37

Where Are Your Forks?

I sat and watched the nurses on the ward for a day. The ward was long and all the supplies were kept at one end in cabinets behind a locked door. Every time there was a need for a bandage, a towel, or a bedpan, a nurse had to leave the patient and walk to the end of the ward, unlock the door, and open multiple cabinets to try and find what was needed. I wondered aloud why everything was kept so far away from where it was used.

"We have some dangerous supplies and drugs on the ward so we have to keep them locked up."

"Does everything have to be locked up, or just the dangerous supplies? What if we placed safe, high-use items closer to where you use them?"

It almost seems like a group of highly trained professionals should have figured that out without being asked, but hold on. This is a common issue and it exists for a good reason. There is so much complexity in jobs today that we relegate as much as possible to habit so we free up the rest of our brain to deal with the constant challenges. Once something is fixed, we leave it there, unless there is some compelling proof that it should be moved.

If something is done 20 times a day and is not set up efficiently, you are wasting time, straining employees, and throwing away money.

It's the same reason your knives, forks, and spoons are in exactly the same drawer they were when you moved in. So, probably, are the rest of the dishes, pans, and spices. It doesn't matter if your needs have changed. Over time you might add new items to your kitchen, but you'll very seldom change the location of the fundamentals.

Even if you move, whoever sets up the kitchen will try to get it similar to the place you left. It might be that you always put the silverware drawer to the right of the dishwasher. This might make sense from an efficiency standpoint, so it goes there. You might put all your cooking utensils in the drawer under the silver and this might also make sense. But what if the new kitchen's stove is placed much further from that drawer than in the old kitchen? Doesn't matter. It's more important that you know where to find the tools.

And, in fact, unless you are disabled in some way, no one is really concerned about the extra steps it takes to make a meal. You only do it occasionally — generally once a day — and no damage is done by those extra steps.

When you get into business though, you see a different problem. If something is done 20 times a day and is not set up efficiently, you are wasting time, straining employees, and throwing away money. This then is a real problem and we have to find a way to solve it.

Any task can be broken down to its most simple steps. But most tasks are anything but simple. They involve false starts, unnecessary steps and backtracking. These extra motions are tiring and cause a frantic pace that makes people even more exhausted than they would be if they just did the work.

The simple answer, to see if you need to change anything, is to do a "spaghetti diagram" of some common tasks. On a single sheet of paper, draw out the floor plan where the task is performed, then put your pen on the paper and track a person's movement as they perform the tasks. If the track they follow looks like spaghetti, or reveals long lines to gather some necessary supply or form, then you have found an area you can improve.

If the task is done once a week, it's probably not going to be high on the list to change. But if it's done regularly throughout the day, the cost of extra steps and effort is much higher than the cost of changing the process and creating new habits.

CHAPTER 38

Hire More "Yes" People

I was consulting for an eastern communications firm when I first saw a positive "yes" person in action. I had heard the old definition of someone who just agrees to get along. This was the first time I'd heard a new definition.

I was an observer at this meeting and would only speak up if invited by the manager. The project room was packed with engineers and programmers working on a tough problem. They were trying to switch from an old technology to a new one in their company. They needed to upgrade operations, make old data available in new systems, and do all this while keeping in mind that their changes would probably have to be updated themselves in a few years.

Most of these meetings were predictable. The company veterans had a tremendous amount of knowledge about how the present system was developed and how it works. Their investment in the status quo meant they also had no interest in change. They were excited about the new opportunities, but they thought it was suicide to change what they had built. They could, themselves, become obsolete.

The "yes" person team approach works because these people have top skills, a clear understanding of the old approaches, and a diplomatic approach to dealing with conflict.

Also at the table would be some new hires who were experts at and advocates of a particular new technology. Their power as technologists was equally matched with their dismal skills at office politics and diplomacy. They were sometimes described as arrogant and abrasive.

Mixed in with this group were some managers who needed to solve the problem, had limited technology knowledge, and were quite willing to knock some heads together to get the job done. These managers would normally try to lead the discussion and problem solving. The other two groups might politely let them try. But the predictable reaction would be to do just what the managers ask, but no more.

I found myself trying to identify who would play which role in the meeting. Some of that could be done by age. The older company employees would probably be on the conservative, protectionist side while the younger would normally be itching for change.

I was wrong. And I was wonderfully wrong about a lot of what I thought would happen next. All because of a "yes" man the manager had hired.

He was hired because he had a few characteristics the manager needed.

He was engaged and a curious problem solver. When faced with a problem his eyes lit up as he faced the challenge.

He appreciated the power of office politics. He knew where real power resided and how to work with power.

He was a technology expert but didn't believe there was one right technology or approach to solve all problems.

He knew how to listen. He appreciated other points of view and could help draw out people's ideas and objections.

Whenever a question about possibility arose, he was more likely to say "Yes, we can do that!," than "No, we've tried that already."

The manager had hired him for just this kind of meeting.

After the manager opened the meeting and laid out his understanding of the problem (and he made it clear that it was likely he didn't understand it completely), he turned the meeting over to the senior technologist.

He was the genius who had kept the company afloat with his knowledge of the outmoded and dying systems. Without him, there would be no company. He spoke about the complexities of tinkering with a complex system. He spoke proudly of how he and his team made repairs, re-wrote ancient code, and anticipated many of the problems and breakdowns from this well-known system. He said he was optimistic about the benefits of a new approach and not quite sure how to go about it.

So far this was standard. But now the "yes" man spoke. He supported everything the senior man said about complex systems and the hidden dangers of even small change. He spoke about a previous project where he had missed important signals and failed. Then he spoke of another project that took those failures into account and described the approach that led to success. There wasn't a pet technology in the discussion.

When the senior technologist had questions or objections ("Sure that worked there, it won't work here because....") the "yes" man took him seriously, wrote down the objections on a flip chart and talked through them.

His deep listening allowed the meeting to progress toward action planning, rather than descend into fear and blame. The actions agreed were small changes on test-bed systems to explore feasibility.

This "yes" person approach works because these people have top skills, a clear understanding of the old approaches, and a diplomatic approach to dealing with conflict. Hiring one or more of them lets you move into the future instead of hanging onto the way it's always been done.

CHAPTER 39

How to Hire an Unqualified Person

My life contains a few instances where I was offered a job even though I didn't make the résumé cut. The best one was when I was hired by Jim Champy of Index to do international business consulting.

I didn't fit the mold at all. Almost everyone there had an advanced degree. They had a lot of experience in their chosen area of expertise and most came to the company with a proven track record.

I had no degree, little obvious experience and I definitely had a track record, just not in any area where Jim's company made their money.

He interviewed me two times. The interviews were more like a conversation. He asked me what I thought on a number of issues, some work-related and some not. He asked very few of the standard questions. Mostly he got to know me and my passions. At the end of the second conversation, he told me I was hired. I had two questions for him.

First, since I had no degree and the firm was full of them, I wondered if that was going to be a problem.

Someone who doesn't meet the academic or experience requirements could actually be the best person for the job.

"Yes," he said, "it will, but only if it is a problem for you. At a certain point, you can either do the work or you can't, and a degree isn't going to make a difference one way or the other."

My second question, now that I was hired, was "What do you want me to do?" He looked at me like I had two heads. "What do I want you to do? I have no idea how to answer that. Here's what I think. You have some good ideas and some passion around those ideas. If there is a market for them, you'll be here for as long as you like. If there is no market, then you'll probably be here about six months. You will have learned something, we will learn something and we'll shake hands and part."

You can imagine that anyone hired with that mandate gets out and gets active in the company.

I made my internal business plan, took everyone I could find out to lunch, starting crafting my offering and got to work. On my first project, I worked with a jazz musician, an IT expert, a nuclear physicist, and an economist. The team was brilliant and innovative because, although we all saw the world in fascinatingly different ways, we were united in the drive to find a solution for our client's problems. That company, full of intelligent misfits, was the best place I ever worked.

It turned out there was a market for what I do, and I stayed with the firm until I left to start my own company.

Our familiar hiring template is designed to eliminate people so we don't have to spend too much time looking at résumés. There will likely be an academic requirement and an experience requirement. Both reasonable, unless we can imagine someone might be excellent in the job without one or both being met.

History is full of people who didn't finish a degree or an advanced degree and yet went on to create outstanding companies or products. We also have many experiences of the outsider coming into a company without specific experience and seeing and acting in the innovative ways required to change the course of a company.

It takes more time, it requires looking between the lines and listening for the kind of person — not the kind of résumé — you want to fill this role. If all hiring fits a standard template, then we're in danger of getting a company full of standard employees. That's not what's needed in our age of competition and innovation.

CHAPTER 40

Do More Performance Reviews

I was sitting with the CEO of an automobile parts company when his contact from HR came to the door. He has an open-door policy so he invited her in and excused himself to talk with her while I listened. She was there to tell him about the revised employee review policy. It didn't go well.

He had asked for a policy that was more effective, easier to use for both employee and reviewer, and something that truly supported their mission.

He listened for a few minutes as she described the new approach. There would be eight total categories of accomplishment, a "speedy" review version that allowed the manager to do an abbreviated version of the review in order to get it done by the deadline, and a more thorough way of incorporating employee feedback into the review. Not bad, but nothing like what he really wanted.

His open-door policy was understood to require fast, no-nonsense communication. She had done her part, now he reciprocated.

"The manager of any employee who isn't meeting expectations is more responsible for that than the employee. If employees can't do the job, they were either a bad hire in the first place or they have been poorly trained or poorly supervised."

"It's too complex. I don't want eight levels of accomplishment. How is anybody supposed to decide between a six or a seven without reading and understanding some pretty fine distinctions? I want three categories — exceeds, meets, or does not meet expectations.

"Then I want each manager to work with each employee to determine those expectations. Employees should have a lot of input on what expectations they are measured against. I want these kinds of reviews done twice a year, but let's be real. If an employee only finds out twice a year how they're doing, they can never really improve. It's the manager's responsibility to keep employees informed on a regular basis how well or how poorly they are doing.

"Here's what you tell people. If you meet expectations you get to keep your job, attend classes that help you improve, and probably get a small raise. When you prove you can regularly meet expectations, you earn a place in one of our planning groups and have the possibility of a larger raise. We understand the value of someone who comes to work every day, works hard, and does well. We don't want to discourage the person who doesn't exceed. They are solidly the backbone of our workforce.

"If you exceed expectations, you are put in a special class of employee who gets a larger voice in the kind of work they do, what kinds of classes they go to, and certainly gets a larger raise. We want you to lead our planning groups and officially help us improve our work and our products.

"If you don't meet expectations, then you have six months to get back into the 'meets' category. And let me make this clear: The manager of any employee who isn't meeting expectations is more responsible for that than the employee. If employees can't do the job, they were either a bad hire in the first place or they have been poorly trained or poorly supervised. If we hire someone for a job, we are stating they can do it and we are stating our commitment to help them do it.

"Also, I want something on the form so the employee can indicate if they were surprised by anything the manager said in the review. Surprises, whether good or bad, are a negative for the manager. All the things the employee needs to know should be known at the moment the manager knows them. Holding them for the big day because they might be uncomfortable is a sign that the manager is not meeting expectations."

The HR person had been writing furiously as the CEO talked. She had just two questions.

"You seriously want reviews done twice a year?"

"Yes."

"What makes you think they'll do it twice a year when we have a hard enough time getting them to do it once?"

"Then they 'do not meet' expectations. Oh, and let's make it clear that our first goal for anyone who cannot meet expectations is to find them a job where they can. If we can find that job inside the plant, that's great. If we can't, then let's expand and find them jobs elsewhere. I want people to know that our first purpose is to make them successful."

And with that, the meeting was over and we went back to our discussion.

CHAPTER 41

No Laughter, No Creativity

I walked into the innovation labs of a food products giant and sat down at the end of a long row of cubicles. I noticed it was quiet, except for the irritating hum of the air handling system.

But the loudest sound was the absence of laughter. Nobody was laughing. I sat there for a couple of hours writing and listening and never once heard laughter. I heard one side of a few phone calls but no conversations. And this was in the innovation lab!

Where there are humans and no laughter, there is only the pretense of life. Especially when we are creating, we are laughing. We laugh because we work together and play together. When that doesn't happen, nothing is created.

When I looked at the new food they offered, I could see results of the lack of innovation. Most were simply variations of current products. Larger or smaller versions, more filling, colored filling, smaller packaging. It looked like innovation, and people bought the new presentations. But the bottom line showed customers bought them in place of the old, not in addition to. They

Most of encouraging your workforce to create involves simply getting out of the way of the natural creativity of humans.

were not building the future company on these retreads.

A few days after this visit, I attended their annual awards ceremony and listened and applauded as PhD after PhD won an award for a patent they had earned for the company. They were certainly creative people, but they weren't innovating. Does that sound strange? The patents were for new chemicals and processes to make the food. They were removing costs and speeding manufacturing, but there was a heavy note behind the applause. I went to talk with some of the award winners after the ceremony and found a group in despair. Almost everyone I spoke with was looking for another job or counting the days until retirement. How could this be? They worked for one of the world's largest companies for good wages and their job was to come up with new ideas. How could it have gotten this bad?

This remarkable collection of people had been driven to despair by the petty rules of an administration who had no idea how to help people innovate.

The air handling system was a perfect example. The loud buzz it made was annoying and distracting. People in the cubicles had requested it be fixed and that fix had been promised. But nothing was done. A company maintenance man had poked around, but what was really needed was an engineer familiar with the system. After a couple of months when nothing was done, the inmates decided they would take over and stop the buzzing. They found a broom, put a towel on the end of it and jammed it up into the fan, stopping it. Eventually, the motor overheated and broke. Buzz fixed.

After the room got hot, the HVAC engineers were called and they discovered and reported the sabotage. People were fired for damaging company property, the engineers repaired the fans which had exactly the same hum and the remaining PhDs kept their brooms out of the ceiling.

In addition to being kept in a long row resembling a prison block, I noticed the cubicles were fairly bland. In most creative shops I'd visited, the creative people took some special pride in making their private space stand out. There was nothing like that here. I asked what was up.

It turned out there were rules about how you could decorate your cubicle. If you wanted a plant, its type and size were controlled. Posters had to be approved. Nothing distracting could appear in the cubicle. "Distracting" was determined by someone who was an

> **To have innovation, to have creativity, you have to have play.**
>
>

administrator and not a PhD. They were specifically forbidden from hanging Dilbert cartoons. Admin enjoyed the power they had over these fancy scientists.

Not having a Dilbert cartoon shouldn't really make a difference in how much someone innovates. But when you add all the petty insults, it's clear that what admin wanted was an obedient creative workforce: an oxymoron.

To create, you have to break the rules. And what they learned was to follow the rules. They learned how to avoid being fired. They colored inside the lines and the company got nothing but safe small changes for their wages.

Most of encouraging your workforce to create involves simply getting out of the way of the natural creativity of humans. You can encourage innovation by making it easier and more acceptable to break the rules, but you can't really administer or manage creativity. And if you want to have creativity, then you have to encourage play.

Play doesn't try to get it right, and it has no problem with failure. To have innovation, to have creativity, you have to have play. It opens the mind and makes people laugh at their mistakes. It's a necessary ingredient, not a frivolous distraction.

There is a lot written about how to make or help people innovate. I think there is a lot of mistaken work on the subject. Given what we have accomplished on the planet, I think it's safe to say that innovation and creativity are our birthright. We are naturally creative if we get the machinery of the corporation out of the way and let nature happen.

Encourage play and individual expression. When done in a context of group success, you can't go wrong.

CHAPTER 42

Do a Succession Action Plan

After the first attacks on the World Trade Center in 1993, former New York Mayor Rudi Giuliani created the Office of Emergency Management. The group spent about $25 million trying to prepare for future city emergencies.

They had many discussions about matching radio frequencies, who would set up and lead incident centers, who would coordinate communication, and so on.

On the morning of the final Trade Center attacks in 2001, it became fatally obvious that all the planning meant nothing in the face of a real crisis. Radios didn't work inside the towers, nobody agreed who was in charge, orders were ignored, and general confusion took over.

A lot of heroic work saved a lot of lives, but the coordination issues lost other lives needlessly. They had bet that a theoretical exercise would work in a real-world crisis.

It's the same with succession planning. If it's done at all, it's usually done too late, with an idealized situation based on best-case conditions. And we never test it.

On the morning of the final Trade Center attacks in 2001 it became fatally obvious that all the planning meant nothing in the face of a real crisis.

Succession planning is meant to keep an organization or department functioning if a key person is removed or diminished. Here are the key things it normally gets wrong.

1. We think of key people as those at the top of the org chart. In fact, many key people don't appear as a name on the org chart. They are a part of a department. They might have key knowledge or play a role in communication that no one else can play.

2. We imagine we will have some warning that the key person is going. We see it as a transition that might occur because of a promotion where we have several weeks' notice. Often an abrupt change due to illness or death or leaving for a new job causes the most problems.

3. We don't clearly identify who will take over for the person who is suddenly not available, and who will take over for *that person* when they move into the key position. Chairs become empty and work gets missed unless we look at succession within the system, rather than in terms of simply replacing one person.

4. We never test it. In my leadership programs, I often see very senior people being bothered all day with tiny decisions that apparently only they can make. In fact, the brief absence of a leader is the best time to test a succession plan. Who will be in charge? What decisions will be prohibited? How well will it last long term?

5. Identification of key people is often poorly done. A lot of organizations struggle and fail to identify people with high potential. The usual suspects show up. We find a lot of men with charisma selected. More quiet men and most women are left out. Yet over and over, I see those people who don't get identified stepping up in emergencies to do the job and lead the team. We need to broaden the definition of high potential.

How should we do it?

Identify key people. Just ask around and discover who would be missed the most, who would affect production the most, if they were suddenly gone.

Meet with those people and tell them what you are doing. Ask them what they think. Listen.

Arrange for each of those people to identify one or two people who could step up right now and handle about 80% of their work.

Arrange for those people to do some shadowing of the key people. Yes, you might have to pay extra to backfill their job while they shadow. That is part of your insurance cost.

Now start sending the key people out of their offices and ask the step-up people to take over. You might send key people on a training or to another internal place to do their own shadowing.

The benefits of this approach go way beyond disaster insurance: You increase cooperation and communication among key contributors.

The resiliency of the entire organization is dramatically increased. The ability of the organization to do its job in a short-term crisis is improved. Bad weather, flu, family emergencies now mean you can continue to operate instead of putting important work on hold.

People feel good about being trained and acknowledged for a larger contribution. These people are more likely to see a future with your organization and stick around.

Be careful not to scare them. Let people know this is for future preparedness, not for replacement. A little awareness that everyone can be replaced is a good thing. Paranoia is not productive.

CHAPTER 43

The Book of Lasts

When my wife was pregnant with our daughter, we bought a small book to record the firsts in her life. Her first real smile, her first word, buying her first shoes. It was fun and it's interesting now to look back at some of the things I've forgotten.

But as I look back, I realize we should have another book. One that's almost impossible to write until long after the fact. That's the book of lasts.

I have photographs of me carrying my daughter on my shoulders. She seemed to have fun up there. It gave her a view from a height even I couldn't attain. Sometimes we'd play and I'd race around making airplane sounds and she'd laugh and laugh.

There came a day when I lifted her onto my shoulders for the last time. I don't even know why it was the last time. I can guess that she grew up and either the weight for me or the dignity for her meant that the next time I went to lift her it didn't happen.

And thinking about that, I thought of how many things in my life happened for the last time and I wasn't aware of the moment.

The last time my son reached for my hand as we crossed the street.

The last time I laughed with a friend before he died of cancer.

The last time my mother said my name.

All these moments came and went without acknowledgment, without celebration or honor. They only become powerful in hindsight.

I don't know what I'd have done differently if I had known the importance of those moments. If I had some view of the future and knew it was a last, would it be right to remark on it? Probably not.

But it would be right to experience in the moment. To slow down and savor the moment when something special is happening. And something special is always happening. Even if we don't realize it's for the last time.

About Ron Donovan

Starting with farm work as an 11-year-old, my working career has taken me around the world and from the factory floor to the CEO tower. I worked in the steel mill where my father spent his life and saw what unions meant, both positive and negative. On the Great Lakes I learned how to keep an iron ore freighter level during loading and unloading — a skill I don't use much anymore.

I started repairing appliances right about the time they changed from being quality investments for a family to being cheap throwaways. Fishing commercially for salmon in the summer in Alaska took a lot of concentration and physical strength. My winter job of building houses in Anchorage provided a feeling of accomplishment at seeing a pile of lumber turned into a house. And that led to my first job as a consultant, after the man whose kitchen I'd remodeled was impressed with my attention to detail.

As the head of fundraising for public television stations I learned how to manage a small staff of professionals and a large staff of volunteers, who were only there because they wanted to be. I really had to improve my management skills to keep them coming back.

As an international consultant, I learned that the smartest people in the room were the employees — the ones doing the actual work. From them I learned to practice the art of the possible. There might be a wonderful theory of how to accomplish something, but if the people doing the work can't or won't employ that theory, it's worse than useless: It's a distraction.

I have also learned that most people in a job truly want to do their best. Too often they are stopped and frustrated by rules, real or imagined, or supervisors who don't know how to help people be their best. I've spent 30 years helping both the managers and frustrated employees improve their work and life satisfaction.

Made in the USA
San Bernardino, CA
11 August 2017